S0-BON-422

Figure Carving in Wood

Human and Animal Forms

Figure Carving in Wood

Human and Animal Forms

Sara Wilkinson

GUILD OF MASTER CRAFTSMAN PUBLICATIONS LTD

First published 2003 by
Guild of Master Craftsman Publications Ltd
Castle Place, 166 High Street, Lewes, East Sussex BN7 1XU

Reprinted 2004

Text and drawings © Sara M. Wilkinson 2003
© in the work GMC Publications 2003

ISBN 1 86108 390 4

All rights reserved

The right of Sara M. Wilkinson to be identified as the author of this
work has been asserted in accordance with the Copyright Designs and
Patents Act 1988, sections 77 and 78.

No part of this publication may be reproduced, stored in a retrieval
system or transmitted in any form or by any means without the prior
permission of the publisher and copyright owner.

This book is sold subject to the condition that all designs are
copyright and are not for commercial reproduction without the
permission of the designer and copyright owner.

The publishers and author can accept no legal responsibility for any
consequences arising from the application of information, advice or
instructions given in this publication.

Whilst every effort has been made to obtain permission from the
copyright holders for all material used in this book, the publishers will
be pleased to hear from anyone who has not been appropriately
acknowledged, and to make the correction in future reprints.

A catalogue record for this book is available from the British Library.

Publisher: Paul Richardson
Art Director: Ian Smith
Production Manager: Stuart Poole
Managing Editor: Gerrie Purcell
Commissioning Editor: April McCroskie
Editor: Stephen Haynes
Designer: Rob Wheele at Wheelhouse Design, Brighton
Photography: GMC Publications/Anthony Bailey: cover, pp. 2, 22,
45, 48, 66, 90, 112, 115, and all photos of author's finished
carvings except pp. 33, 40, 104 (by Sara Wilkinson);
Donald Simpson: p. 8, p. 11 bottom right; Keith Barker:
pp. 12, 18; V&A Picture Library: pp. 13–17; Roger Wolfe: p. 19;
Chloe Battle: p. 20; all others by Sara Wilkinson
Picture researcher: Kylie Johnston

Set in Sabon and Cygnet

Colour origination by Viscan Graphics Pte Ltd, Singapore
Printed and bound by Kyodo Printing Co Pte Ltd, Singapore

Contents

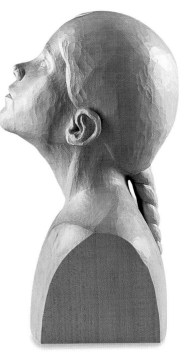

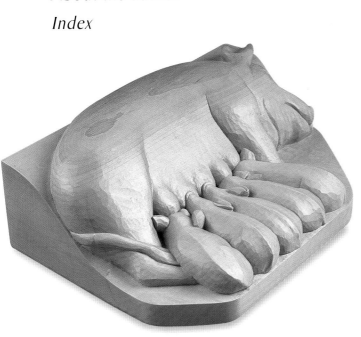

For Chris and Florence

Acknowledgements

I would like to thank the following for their help, encouragement and assistance in producing this book: Christopher Reid and Florence Wilkinson for their kind support, Stephen Haynes of GMC Publications for his editorial expertise, and sculptors Donald Simpson and Donald Potter for allowing me to show their work. For assistance of various kinds in producing photographs I would like to thank Donald Simpson, Keith Barker of Exeter cathedral, Geoffrey Day and the Warden and Scholars of Winchester College, Roger Wolfe of St John's College, York, the Reverend Canon Woods of Sherborne Abbey, the Reverend Martin Clarke of Stowlangtoft church, Vivienne Light, Sarah Jackson and Gordon Hawley.

Safety

Woodcarving should not be a dangerous activity, provided that sensible precautions are taken to avoid unnecessary risk.

♦ Always ensure that work is securely held in a suitable clamp or other device, and that the workplace lighting is adequate.

♦ Keep tools sharp; blunt tools are dangerous because they require more pressure and may behave unpredictably. Store them so that you, and others, cannot touch their cutting edges accidentally.

♦ Be particular about disposing of shavings, finishing materials, oily rags, etc., which may be a fire hazard.

♦ Do not work when your concentration is impaired by drugs, alcohol or fatigue.

♦ Do not remove safety guards from power tools such as angle grinders; pay attention to electrical safety.

♦ It is not safe to use a chainsaw without the protective clothing which is specially designed for this purpose, and attendance on a recognized training course is strongly recommended. Be aware that regulations governing chainsaw use are revised from time to time.

♦ The safety advice in this book is intended for your guidance, but cannot cover every eventuality: the safe use of hand and power tools is the responsibility of the user. If you are unhappy with a particular technique or procedure, do not use it – there is always another way.

Measurements

Although care has been taken to ensure that the imperial measurements are true and accurate, they are only conversions from metric; they have been rounded up or down to the nearest ⅛in, or to the nearest convenient equivalent in cases where the metric measurements themselves are only approximate. When following the projects, use either the metric or the imperial measurements; do not mix units.

Introduction

Nothing is more exciting than working one's way into a lump of timber and releasing a recognizable shape using nothing but hand tools. It satisfies a very primitive instinct – to create just for the love of the material and the absorption and concentration involved in the making processes.

My aim in writing this book is to show how you can carve figures and animals by using your own material (ideas, drawings and photographs) with confidence, rather than copying other carvers' work. You can even carve portraits of your family and pets, as I have done. Although I describe the making of some of my carvings in detail, I hope that you will use these purely as examples, rather than trying to reproduce them.

I discuss all the tools, timber and equipment needed for figure carving, but I have not gone into basic subjects such as the use of tools, or sharpening techniques. If you have never held a carving gouge before, there are already several excellent books for beginners which will start you off with the mechanics (see 'Further reading', page 114). This book is intended for those who have some skill or knowledge already and, having tried some basic projects in the round, now want to work independently and progress to something a little more challenging and individual.

I have gone into great detail on preparation before carving. Obviously there is great enjoyment to be had in just hacking away at a piece of wood and seeing what emerges, but if you want to carve someone or something specific and in a certain style, then I personally think there is a need to prepare the work properly. Many novice carvers are so enthusiastic at the idea of starting a carving that they think of preparation as a loss of valuable carving time, without realizing that the more time you spend planning *before* you start carving, the more efficient you are when using the tool. By careful preparation – drawing, photography, researching, considering style, and really *looking* at your subject – you become so immersed in it that when you come to start carving you can actually *see* your carving in the block (believe me!). Chips fly from your tool at twice the speed. No more staring at the piece of wood wondering where to begin and which bits to knock off next – each section flows seamlessly into the next. That is the theory, anyway – and with time it'll be practice, too.

I use no electrical equipment in figure and animal carvings, other than to bandsaw the outline at the beginning. Obviously you can remove mass quickly with an angle grinder and produce more detail with rotary shafts if you prefer – there is no right or wrong – but personally I like no dust and no sound other than the tap of mallet on tool and my own choice of music to work to.

CHAPTER 1
Looking at carvings

I would advise any potential (or existing) figure carver to spend as much time as possible looking at examples of carving in the round by different sculptors and carvers, past and present. This will help you to develop an eye for design, and an awareness of the possibilities and limitations of carving in wood. By looking at other people's work, you will form a clearer idea of what you wish to achieve or avoid in your own carving. Though books are an invaluable source of reference, there is no substitute for seeing the actual carving in real life.

Many countries have national or regional museums where a complete cross section of historical work can be seen. In England, for example, the most available selection must be that of the Victoria and Albert Museum in London. Many smaller museums throughout the country have their own collections, and there are specialist galleries dedicated to specific sculptors, such as Barbara Hepworth and Henry Moore. Works by these and other noted twentieth-century sculptors of wood and stone, as well as earlier works, can be seen in the major public galleries. Private galleries frequently have exhibitions of sculpture, and there is a growing number of craft shows, fairs and carving exhibitions (of varying quality), with carvers demonstrating their skills. Some important collections in other countries are listed under 'Some places to visit' on page 114.

In this chapter I will focus on ecclesiastical figurative carving, as historically it was religious institutions that provided the most employment for carvers, and they still have the best examples of work to be seen. First I will look at medieval churches, and then at individual pieces, mainly from the Victoria and Albert Museum.

Monk reading
Oak
Choir stall,
Sherborne Abbey,
Dorset

Church carving

If you enjoy exploring, there is a wealth of beautiful woodcarving readily available for us to see, still in the settings for which it was intended, in cathedrals and parish churches the length and breadth of Britain and other European countries. (It is only for the sake of convenience that I have taken most of my examples from the eastern counties of England, where I live.) Most country churches are accessible to the public – they may be left unlocked, or there may be a keyholder nearby – although some are tucked away in remote and isolated little villages and no longer used for worship.

When these churches were built, they played a central role in the lives of the parishioners. The church's power and importance were reflected in the wealth of skill that was employed in the building and decoration. Initially the woodcarver was very much subservient to the mason, but as the carved screens and ornament in wood became more elaborate, the woodcarver became more independent and was recognized as a skilled craftsman in his own right. Oak, either home-grown or imported, was plentiful in Britain at this time, and its strength and robust character made it ideal for furnishing the interiors of churches.

What makes medieval carving so relevant and interesting to the modern carver is that the tools used in this period were pretty much identical to the tools we use today, if somewhat heavier. In Hannover museum in Germany there is a choir-stall panel in deep relief, dated 1285, of a seated monk busily carving at a small bench, holding a round mallet, such as we use now, and a carving gouge. On the wall, carved behind, hang a row of gouges in different sweeps, a try square and some callipers: we could step straight into his workshop and take over now.

Choir stalls

When most of our churches were built, it was expected that the worshippers would stand or kneel, and so seating was not provided, except for stone benches around the walls for the old and infirm. Wooden seating first appeared in the cathedrals and larger churches as choir stalls for monks, priests and clerks who had to spend several hours at a time at prayer.

Cherry seller
Oak
Choir stall,
Sherborne Abbey,
Dorset

Frequently these choir stalls were elaborately carved with fine canopies and tracery, some culminating in arches and spires. In complete contrast to this lofty carving, lower down, at a more human level, the arm supports often featured a little carving: a figure or head, grotesque or animal, called an 'elbow'. Their purpose appears to be purely ornamental, although perhaps they were intended as useful little handles for pulling oneself up from a seated position. Most of them certainly seem to be nicely rounded and smooth, as if to fit into the palm of the hand. The beautifully compact examples (opposite and above) of the cherry seller and the reading monk, seated comfortably on his cushion, are from Sherborne Abbey in Dorset, England. For figures this small, and especially when carved in oak, the detail is very fine; the monk's face, with his look of deep concentration, is especially expressive.

Heads, such as this one from Stowlangtoft in Suffolk (above right), abound in East Anglian churches; many sport idiosyncratic headgear. This man's hair and beard drape beautifully around the frame of the choir-stall arm. What these three examples have in common is that they are well-designed little figures, with no unnecessary vulnerable pieces to break off.

Male head
Oak
Choir stall,
Stowlangtoft,
Suffolk

5

Angel and scroll
Oak
Misericord,
Stowlangtoft,
Suffolk

Misericords

Each of the choir stalls contained a wooden seat known as a 'misericord' (from the Latin *misericordia*, meaning 'mercy'). This is a hinged or pivoted flap which, in the upright position, provides a little ledge on which the clergy could perch during those parts of the service when they were required to stand. Misericords are carved from one thick slab of oak, including the ledge and its wedge-shaped central support. It is the wealth of skilful and imaginative carving found on these supports which is of such interest. Although strictly speaking these

carvings are in deep relief, rather than in the round, they are so deeply worked as to provide many examples of three-dimensional figure and animal carvings.

Carved misericords are not confined to Britain – France, in particular, has many fine examples. The oldest complete set in Britain is to be found in Exeter cathedral, where most are believed to have been carved between 1220 and 1250, by one man – although many cathedrals and large churches have sets which are well worth looking at. As with the carved bench ends, misericords represent a study of all aspects of medieval life, with subjects as diverse as

6

decorative foliage; real, imaginary and grotesque animals; biblical scenes; allegories; romances; and scenes from everyday life. Amongst the latter, trades, hunting, fights between husbands and wives, bawdiness and ale consumption are favourite subjects, often depicted with humour and wit.

As far as the quality of the carving is concerned, naturally they vary from the crude to the highly skilled; some show a sophisticated sense of perspective and design. Most of them share a robust and chunky style (although often finished with fine detail), suited to their purpose of supporting human weight, as well as to amuse, instruct, entertain and provoke thought. Because the carving was safely hidden beneath the seat, many have survived intact.

These two examples, again from Stowlangtoft in Suffolk, illustrate a perfect balance between a bold shape and crisply cut detail. The angel's hair, clothing and wings are all worked with different tooled finishes which together form a pleasing unity; the eagle has a very finely carved head and feathers, with the tail swept up to join the wing so as to create the desired compact shape.

Eagle and scroll
Oak
Misericord,
Stowlangtoft,
Suffolk

Bench ends

RIGHT
Lady with dog
Oak
Bench end, Ixworth
Thorpe, Suffolk

BELOW
Thatcher with tools
Oak
Bench end, Ixworth
Thorpe, Suffolk

In the fourteenth century wooden seating for ordinary people began to be provided, and by the fifteenth it became widespread. Initially the seats were long boards of oak with plain slabs of wood for the bench ends, but during the fifteenth century the ends became much more embellished and elaborately shaped, with the woodcarver very much

in demand. In England, the West Country specialized in relief-carved square ends, whereas East Anglia abounds in 'poppyheads' (from the French word *poupée*, meaning a puppet or figurehead). Many of these poppyheads are finished with foliage, but some have charmingly depicted little figures, heads or animals carved alongside.

As with the misericords, some of the figures are concerned with daily labours, some are humorous and others have a biblical or moral theme. These photographs show three such figures, two of which – the thatcher and the noblewoman with her dog – are in

Bagpiper
Oak
Bench end,
Honington, Suffolk

Ixworth Thorpe church in Suffolk, while the bagpipe player is in nearby Honington. They were clearly worked by the same hand, sharing similar features and dress and the same compact style, and all three stand or sit astride the bench end, to the side of the poppyhead.

Wilby church in Suffolk is unusual in that it has many little group carvings, such as the two examples below. One depicts a baptism, but the meaning of the other appears unclear. (I cannot help thinking that it looks like a film shoot, with the figure on the right holding a clapperboard.)

Baptism group, *Oak*
Bench end, Wilby, Suffolk

Unidentified group, *Oak*
Bench end, Wilby, Suffolk

The same church also has some nice little individual figures, like this man with his horse, and the other of a man with what I imagine to be a wine flagon.

During the Reformation of the early sixteenth century many figures were defaced or destroyed in European churches, as they were considered idolatrous. Sadly, many churches in East Anglia have headless figures at their pew ends, which makes for a melancholy visit when one happens upon them unexpectedly in a disused church – as if life past and present has been erased from what was once the centre of the village.

However, coming across the wonderful animal carvings in Stowlangtoft is a very different experience. The medieval carver was quite happy to mix realism with total fantasy and create hybrid creatures, which often had a meaning to their

ABOVE
Man with packhorse
Oak
Bench end,
Wilby, Suffolk

RIGHT
Man with flagon or
wineskin
Oak
Bench end,
Wilby, Suffolk

contemporaries which is lost to us now. Shown here are a very credible spaniel or water dog, with loose locks of fur, a wonderfully incongruous image of a boar playing the harp, and one of three or four carvings with bird bodies and human heads. A visit to this church certainly makes one wonder why most modern animal carvers want to stick so rigidly to realism – what has happened to our imagination over the centuries?

RIGHT
Spaniel, *Oak*
Bench end, Stowlangtoft, Suffolk

BELOW
Boar playing the harp, *Oak*
Bench end, Stowlangtoft, Suffolk

BELOW RIGHT
Owl man, *Oak*
Bench end, Stowlangtoft, Suffolk

Annunciation to the shepherds. *Oak*
Exeter cathedral

Occasionally one comes across isolated figures or groups, such as this charming example from Exeter cathedral, which is the only remaining section of a larger Nativity scene. In spite of its seeming simplicity, it is cleverly composed. The angel, from the angle of his body, appears to be flying down from on high, although in actuality he is carved alongside the earthbound shepherd beside him. The story is all clearly there for the onlooker to see, from the angel carrying his message, to the expectant look on the faces of the shepherds. Wood is put to admirable use with the sheep (carved a little small) climbing up a hillock in the foreground. This pulls the whole composition together into a tight unity, with no vulnerable pieces or superfluous detail.

Figures and groups from the Victoria and Albert Museum

Unlike the church carvings described above – which, apart from the Nativity scene, are all *in situ* – the following works are no longer to be seen in the position for which they were carved, and therefore we tend to look at them as separate entities, rather than as a small part of a whole building. The Reformation was responsible for mass destruction in Protestant countries, with most of the statuary demolished: therefore, to see the full wealth of larger early European woodcarving in place, we have to travel to mainland Europe, and especially those parts of Germany which remained Catholic. However, the Victoria and Albert Museum has some very fine pieces from different countries.

The style of the English oak carvings contrasts greatly with that of the German limewood carvers working in the fifteenth and sixteenth centuries, who elevated their craft to a high art form through their altarpieces and statuary, with breathtaking realism, detail and complexity. Of these German carvers, Tilman Riemenschneider (1460–1531) could be considered the master.

I have selected these examples not just for the superb technical skill and composition portrayed in them, but also for the sense of empathy created by the carvers, which one feels when looking at each work.

Group carvings

The group of Mary Salome and Zebedee, carved from one piece of lime by Riemenschneider around 1520, and its companion carving now in Stuttgart, are thought to have been originally placed either side of an altarpiece depicting the Holy Kindred. However, we have to view the carving, now separated, as an individual work, as seen in the museum. It still makes a complete and interesting group carving in its own right.

Although an ecclesiastical carving, this work has a secular air: the clothing is that of fashionable Germany of the time, and the books give the impression of an evening spent peacefully reading, rather than of a biblical scene. The skill of the carver is immediately obvious, but what to me is even more impressive is the feeling of tranquillity created in the piece

by the homely setting, the relaxed air of the man, and the placid features of both.

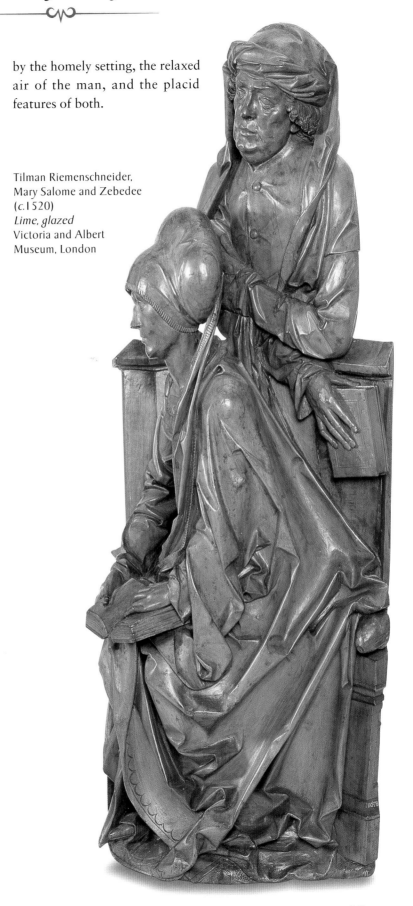

Tilman Riemenschneider,
Mary Salome and Zebedee
(c.1520)
Lime, glazed
Victoria and Albert
Museum, London

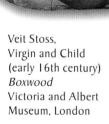

From exactly the same period is a boxwood carving (left) by another leading German carver, Veit Stoss (*c*.1445–1533). The most extraordinary thing about this carving on first viewing, especially after one has seen it reproduced in books, is its diminutive size. The whole piece is no more than 200mm (8in) high, making the tiny Christ about 40mm (1½in) in length. Boxwood is, of course, the most suitable wood for miniature carving, but we must still marvel at Stoss's skill at detail; though perhaps the exaggerated drapery is a little overworked for modern tastes.

Compact, detailed carvings in box and pearwood of both religious and secular themes, produced in the Netherlands, became fashionable amongst private collectors from about 1520 onwards. The south Netherlandish example (*c*.1525–50) of two mourning women, carved in boxwood, is a beautiful example of this style.

Figure carving

As with the group of Mary Salome and Zebedee, which is without its companion carving, so the French fifteenth-century figure of the angel Gabriel (opposite) must be looked at in isolation, without the Virgin whom he would have been addressing. Although originally completely painted and gilded (and very fine it must have looked, too), it has lost much of its colour. However, it is so sensitively and elegantly carved that despite being made of oak – rather than lime or box, which take more detail – the carving still looks good where the paint has gone. Every fold, feather and lock of hair combine to give a pleasing and balanced unity to this carving, and the angel's stance and expression both give him authority and yet at the same time make him approachable – entirely suitable for the task of delivering his message to the unseen Virgin.

Veit Stoss,
Virgin and Child
(early 16th century)
Boxwood
Victoria and Albert
Museum, London

Netherlandish school,
Two Marys (16th century),
Boxwood
Victoria and Albert Museum,
London

French school,
Angel of the
Annunciation
(*c.1415–50*)
*Oak, painted
and gilt*
Victoria and Albert
Museum, London

Head of a girl, attributed to
Michel or Gregor Erhart (*c.*1500)
Lime
Victoria and Albert Museum, London

Two portraits

These limewood heads of around 1500
are again German, and have been
attributed variously to Michel Erhart
(*fl.* 1469–1522) and to his son Gregor
(*fl.* 1495–1525), who was working in
a similar style. They are thought to
represent the heads of saints, although
they are clearly drawn from the life, and
were possibly produced as models for
goldsmiths' work.

Seen together, these two heads
complement each other in style and
feeling, both sharing a gentle and

Head of a youth, attributed to
Michel or Gregor Erhart (*c.*1500)
Lime
Victoria and Albert Museum, London

expressive countenance. The girl has an open, clear face and smooth forehead, with her hair drawn back, and the carver has managed to capture the impression that she is just on the brink of uttering something, with her lips parted, revealing her teeth and tongue. The youth appears to be listening, with a look of concentration about his eyes. His smoothly worked face is framed by a head of vigorously carved shaggy curls. As portraits in wood, they must be as near perfection as one could imagine.

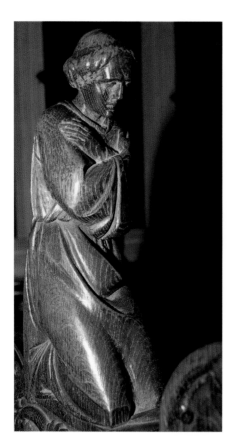

Ethiopian eunuch
(19th century)
Oak
Bench end,
Exeter cathedral

Kneeling figure
(19th century)
Oak
Bench end,
Exeter cathedral

Later church woodcarving

In the Catholic countries of Europe the tradition of ecclesiastical statuary and carving continued unabated. With the rise of Protestantism in Britain, however, that tradition fell into decline. Very few new churches were built until after the Great Fire of London (1666), when Wren's and Hawksmoor's famous churches of classical design dominated the London skyline. With the notable exception of Grinling Gibbons (1648–1721), whose magnificent limewood angels and cherubs adorn the choir stalls and organ cases in St Paul's cathedral, wood as a sculptural material played a secondary role. Stone and marble were seen as far grander and more stately materials, both within the church, and

even more so in the great rise of secular sculpture in the seventeenth and eighteenth centuries. Obviously, large statues and monuments which were to be situated outside needed to be made of stone, but the finer qualities of marble and the malleability of terracotta were generally favoured over the humbler qualities of wood for privately commissioned portraits and busts as well. Even Gibbons, Britain's finest woodcarver, used wood mainly for decorative work, preferring stone and marble for figure and monumental carving.

Wood did, however, regain some importance in Victorian times with the Gothic revival, when many churches were refitted or new ones built. Victorian carving is sometimes regarded as inferior to medieval carving, perhaps because many examples were reproduced in medieval style but with something missing (often humour), or because the copies were a little over-careful and studied-looking. This is in fact a rather unfair assessment, as there was much fine carving produced at this time. The replacement choir-stall ends (opposite), from a complete set in Exeter cathedral representing biblical themes, have a quiet, solemn air, in keeping with Victorian tastes.

By the early twentieth century, leading sculptors such as Henry Moore, Barbara Hepworth and Eric Gill were working in wood as well as stone. This helped to give wood some respectability in the art world, rather than being seen purely as a craft material. Also, subject matter became freer as sculptors had the opportunity to design and produce work to sell in galleries, rather than having to stick rigidly to the constraints imposed by patrons; therefore the boundaries between ecclesiastical and secular carving became more blurred.

The two figures below, representing Church and Synagogue, were commissioned in the early twentieth century by St John's College in York for their chapel. They were carved in oak by Alan Durst in a lively, and yet to some eyes rather unfinished, style. Although this style is in perfect keeping with the medieval tradition, in no way do these figures feel like reproductions: rather, they are very good examples of work of their period. The emphasis in these figures is on their imposing form, used to convey a message, rather than on over-finished detail.

Alan Durst, Synagogue (early 20th century)
Oak
Chapel of St John's College, York

Alan Durst, Church (early 20th century)
Oak
Chapel of St John's College, York

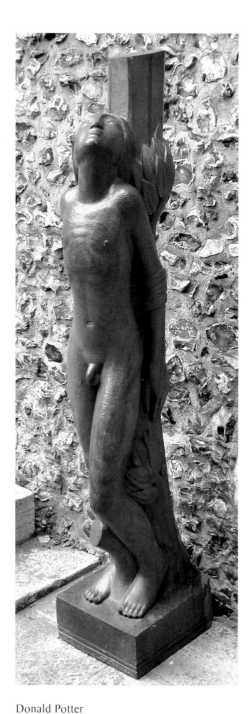

Donald Potter
(after Eric Gill),
St Sebastian
(20th century)
Walnut
Winchester College
Library

This walnut figure of the martyred St Sebastian, carved by Donald Potter after a sketch by Eric Gill, is an extremely fine example of figure carving from the first half of the twentieth century. The piece is simple, yet slightly stylized. Obvious symbolism and clues to the story (such as the many arrows traditionally depicted) are kept to a minimum, the bound arms and uplifted face being all that is necessary to impart the religious theme. A beautifully executed tooled finish contrasts with the two previous carvings, and with the next one.

20

Donald Simpson's crucifix, carved from holly in the 1950s, is even more sparse in style, but with a warmth and smoothness of finish made possible by the pale, close-grained nature of the timber. Shape and form, rather than detail, had become the overriding force in twentieth-century figurative carving.

By looking back through the centuries, carvers working today can draw inspiration from hundreds of years of figure carving, while developing a style of their own.

Donald Simpson, Crucifix (mid-20th century)
Holly

CHAPTER 2

Preparation

The first step in preparing for carving is to consider what you want to carve – in our case a person or animal – and what you want to carve it out of – wood. In order to make a representation of an animate object out of an inanimate material, you must understand the nature of both: you have the task of portraying a complex human or animal form out of a hard mass.

Importance of anatomy

The living form is composed of skeleton, muscle, flesh and skin, with hair, feather or fur as appropriate (the internal organs are not usually of much interest to carvers). Make yourself familiar with how bodies look, work and move. For general understanding, a good book of anatomy is essential if you aim to take the subject seriously. Making drawings and photographs, as well as simply looking at the actual person or creature, is equally important. The human form is especially difficult to represent, as it is so familiar and yet so complex: we have no fur or feather to hide behind, and we're familiar with the shape yet unfamiliar with the structure. It is easy to spot what is wrong with a bad figure carving, and yet difficult to do it correctly. Conversely, opposite problems arise when carving animals: we are generally less familiar with the subject itself. Too often, carvings are started with an inadequate knowledge of the form of the animal, which is then disguised by detailed feathers or fur. Do not make the mistake of thinking that knowledge of anatomy is unimportant because you wish to simplify your figure: it is still necessary to study proportion and form. This is of course also true if you wish to conceal most of the figure in clothing.

Next, consider the material you'll be working with. Unless you are very experienced, do not try to be over-ambitious. Remember that wood has its limitations and that vulnerable pieces carved from short grain are liable to break off. I will be discussing suitable timber in more detail later in this chapter.

Also remember that the *form* of the carving is the main consideration in good design, rather than detail. The carving must do what you want it to do, whether it is to be bold, shocking, whimsical, realistic, stylized or abstract.

The subject

If you choose as your model a person (or a domestic animal) who is well known to you, you will find it much easier than using a photograph or drawing of an unknown person. Not only can you study their mannerisms, expressions and characteristics with a view to incorporating these into your carving, but you can also view them from different angles. They will probably be willing to pose for you, and you can always ask them to stand still for a few minutes while you study them during carving. My daughter Florence, aged seven or eight, got so fed up with me asking her to model that she started charging me five pence each time she had to stand still. However, it was worth it: I was able to study my subject, and she got richer.

If you can sketch, you have a head start. Drawing is a necessary part of carving, and a pencil should come to hand as readily as a carving tool. Make as many drawings as possible so that you become totally familiar with your subject, remembering to draw from different angles. This will make you really *look* at your subject; you will be surprised to discover so many things you don't normally notice about those with whom you live. An ideal preparation would be to go to life-drawing classes. However, you may not feel confident enough to rely on your drawings alone, and you cannot expect children and

Heads should be photographed from a variety of angles, using a reasonably long lens if possible

animals to stay still for long or to be keen on posing again and again for you to draw them. Carving is extremely time-consuming, and the sitter would have to put in many patient hours for you. Therefore, by far the easiest method of recording your subject is to take photographs and make simple scale drawings from these afterwards.

Using photographs

Collecting a bank of photographs for reference is an extremely helpful aid for checking proportions and the structure of the body. If you can take different views of the subject your work will be made far easier. Although it is possible to produce

a good carving from one view only, you must have a sound grasp of anatomy and be able to visualize an all-round image in your head. The front view presents no problems, but what about the sides and back? How thick are the limbs and torso compared with their width? By having your bank of photographs to use in conjunction with a good book of anatomy – and preferably some practice in drawing – you should be well prepared before you begin the carving process.

Taking portrait photographs for reference

Take more photographs than you think you need. It is a false economy to skimp

Children are best photographed from their own level, rather than from above

on film, as you often only get half a dozen usable shots from a roll. The background is, in a sense, unimportant, but try to have as little distraction in the background as possible. Remember, your photographs are simply to record the subject; the aim is not to make beautiful pictures. It is best to take your photos outside, so that you do not have to use a flash and can stand far enough away. Take the photos in bright shade or on a bright overcast day; otherwise, if the subject has their back to the sun they will appear in silhouette, or, if they face the sun, they will squint. If you have to take the photos inside, the natural light from

a well-lit window is preferable to the harshness of flash lighting.

To take successful shots, stand some distance away from your subject and, if possible, use a long or 'portrait' lens. If you stand too close you will get foreshortening – in other words, the person's legs will seem disproportionately short compared with the upper part of the body and head. If you wish to keep a bank of photographs for reference and for measuring proportions, get the person to rotate 90° each time so that you get front, back and side shots.

A variety of angles is especially important in taking photographs of heads, where you need good views of the features from front and side. It is difficult for the subject to look relaxed and not self-conscious when having their face photographed. It is perhaps easier for them to focus their eye on a bush or something behind you, rather than on you yourself – and remember not to have them looking towards the sun, as the squinting will distort the features. A large aperture on the camera will blur the background so that it is not too distracting. I took the shots on pages 24–5 with a zoom lens so that, although it looks as if I'm very close to the subject, I could get close-up shots without the distortion which would be caused by a genuinely close viewpoint.

When taking photographs of children, either stand them on a chair so that your central viewpoint is in the middle rather than looking down at them, or else kneel down to their level. It is also the case, when photographing seated adults, that you too should be seated so that you are at the same level.

Photographing animals

Similarly, if you wish to photograph your favourite rabbit or pet poodle, remember to place them on a table first and take all four views, keeping your camera level with the animal. You could also lie down on your stomach and take your photos looking directly towards the animal; however, it is likely to run towards you unless someone else attracts its attention. Do not sit your dog on the floor and then take a photograph looking straight down at it, or the head will be enormously out of proportion with the feet.

I have people in classes who insist that their photograph – like this one – is

A high viewpoint will distort the proportions of an animal

entirely accurate, and want to draw around the photograph to carve. It is true that this is what the dog looks like when you stand alongside and look down at it, yet if you start measuring the head in proportion to the legs you will soon realize the effect of foreshortening.

If you wish to carve larger domestic animals, open farms, where the animals can wander freely, provide many obliging models. I took these photographs at a local rescue farm, where the animals are especially docile and obligingly posed as I squatted down and took their front, side and back portraits.

Studies of a tame animal from different directions are an invaluable source of reference

ABOVE
The eye-level viewpoint makes this picture especially useful

RIGHT
This spontaneous photograph inspired the carving shown on page 76

These cockerels were sitting on a mound of rubbish, the better to crow, and therefore I was able to photograph them at eye level.

More interesting poses

Of course, the portrait method is not spontaneous, however, and the subject can appear very stiff. Do you really want to carve a person who is standing stock-still with their hands by their sides? Such photographs are invaluable as references for proportion and for studying muscles, etc., but usually the best, most natural poses are one-offs, as in the case of the girl with the duck, opposite.

How often are you lucky enough to get a child – or a bird or animal – to pose so elegantly on their own, let alone both together? However, obviously one can only photograph a front view in a pose like this: if you move to the side, either the child or the duck will move or turn to look at you. The carving which resulted from this photograph is shown in detail in Chapter 4 (pages 76–81).

Altering the subject for carving

Photography is tricky, however, and sometimes you have the idea, the subject and the timber ready but the photo doesn't look quite as you want. If you look at the photograph opposite, the idea is good, the ducks look great, but the child looks awkward – which is hardly surprising, holding two heavy ducks.

I simply re-posed the child, this time holding teddy bears. These were lighter and easier to hold, so she relaxed and had a more serene expression. I then had two photos to use, which, although each was insufficient on its own, together could be used to make a drawing for carving.

LEFT
No animals were harmed in the making of this book!

RIGHT
Girl with ducks
Lime
The comfortable stance of the finished carving was obtained by posing the child with lightweight toys

33

A reference collection of different facial expressions

Do not forget that unless you are carving a portrait you do not have to slavishly copy your model. Your drawings or photographs are a reference for proportion, pose and the way clothes hang, for example. You can dress your model up as you like if they're happy to pose for you. I like to keep most of my

carvings simple, but if you wish to carve a figure with robes, for example, the folds of material will be far more lifelike if you can study how they actually fall on a person, rather than trying to imagine them.

You might also wish your model to pose various facial expressions rather than staying totally relaxed. This, of course, depends on the finished carving you envisage.

Alternative sources for inspiration

If you cannot find a suitable model or do not feel confident in taking your own photographs, you can of course use images from books, magazines or newspapers. Sometimes you see a pose that catches your eye, taken by a professional photographer, which is perfect for carving. I have a bit of a purist streak which tells me that it is not really my own project in that case, but of course that is rubbish – it is still your interpretation of the image. One of my figure carvings was prompted by a photograph from a newspaper which was advertising a photographic exhibition, because I liked the way the girl was standing – although in the event I changed everything about her except the pose.

If you wish to carve animals that do not live with you – a bison or boa constrictor, for instance – there are excellent photographs in children's encyclopedias and in wildlife and bird magazines. Black and white photographs of animals are often more useful than colour pictures, as they encourage you to focus more on the shape, rather than being distracted by changes of colour in fur and feathers. Farms, zoos and country fairs are also good places to make sketches or take photographs for carving animals. Watching wildlife programmes also helps in noting anatomy and how animals move. Try not to copy other people's poor drawings, as you will only magnify their mistakes.

Do not be fooled into thinking that good photographs or drawings are unnecessary for a simple or stylized animal carving. On the contrary, sound research is even more essential if the animal is simplified, as every line must be telling and relevant: you have no fussy detail to hide behind.

Drawing from imagination

If you are skilled at drawing or have a set idea in your head, there is nothing, of course, to stop you from simply drawing straight onto paper or even onto your piece of wood, without any photographs or sketches from life. As long as you have a good sense of anatomy and the style you envisage, then this should not be a problem. Life-drawing classes are the best way to improve your drawing skills and brush up on your anatomy. Remember that you can always refer to your bank of photographs when you need to check proportions.

Style

Consider the style of your carving. Are you intending to carve a realistic, representational figure, or something in a freer style? You might wish to simplify detail and think more in terms of form instead, and this might be reflected in your final drawing. Drawing helps to make you think more about the kind of carving you want to achieve. You might wish to elongate limbs and make an elegant shape, or you might want a chunky, solid-looking carving.

RIGHT
Standing nude
Oak
The pose – though nothing else – was suggested by a published photograph

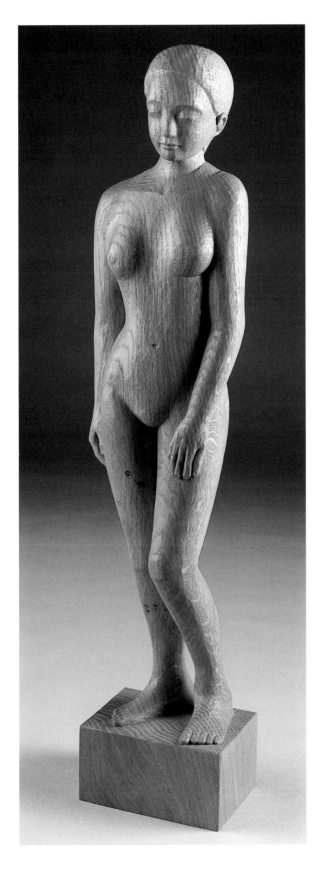

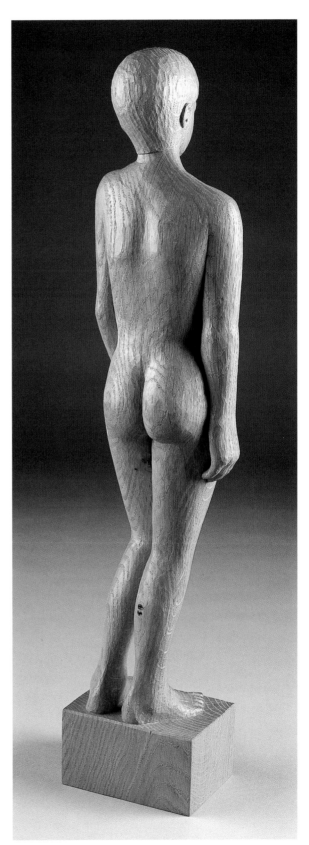

Drawing up for carving

Unless you like carving on a very small scale, it is unlikely that your photos will be large enough to transfer the measurements straight onto your wood. You can, of course, have your photos enlarged, or take a photocopy and have it blown up, but it is very good practice to draw up a pencil outline yourself. Do not worry about putting in all the detail – it is the form and dimensions with which we are concerned at this stage. Work out how many times larger than the photographic image you wish to make your carving. This will usually be fixed by the size of timber available, unless you are willing to join sections. I tend to keep my drawing to a simple pencil outline on paper and then draw like mad on the wood during carving; but you may wish to add shading, on paper, so as to create a more three-dimensional image.

The maquette

A maquette is a model which you can make of your intended carving to help you to visualize it three-dimensionally. It is usually made of clay or some proprietary modelling material such as Plasticine, with a wire support and attached to a wooden base if necessary. I have read several arguments for and against making a maquette.

On the 'for' side, it really can help you to observe solid mass and proportion, and is particularly useful to those who find difficulty in 'seeing' their figure in a lump of wood before they start. Some people like to actually feel the shape with their fingers, and can then more readily visualize which bits to remove. In the past, maquettes were frequently made by artists so that they could pass their designs on to carvers to execute, rather than undertaking this process themselves.

In the 'against' camp, purists argue that as the processes are opposite – that is, in the model you are building up from a *plastic* (malleable) material, whereas woodcarving involves the removal of solid material – the two should not be mixed in technique or style. They believe that a woodcarving should not resemble a clay sculpture, as the two call for different treatments. In making a clay figure, you can sometimes forget that wood has more limitations than your lump of clay. Do not forget that thin limbs, for example, are fine in pottery, but when designing for wood, short grain must be taken into account (see the next section). By carving directly into the wood, you are closer to the original subject: the maquette creates another step, distancing the finished carving from the subject.

Personally, I have rarely made a maquette, but you can decide for yourself whether you would find it useful. If you do, concentrate on form and keep it simple: you are not trying to make a beautifully finished model, just a useful working aid.

Timber and equipment for figure carving

If you are going to carve a figure which takes many hours to produce, it is essential to use a piece of timber that you are happy with. Using any old scrap of wood is a false economy and will ruin the appearance of the finished work. The cost of timber is negligible compared with the labour.

Wood or idea first?

Some carvers start with a piece of timber and then decide what to carve from it; others start with an idea and then look for a piece of timber. You might live with a bit of wood for years and then imagine a carving sitting inside it, or else you might have a commission and have to seek out a suitable piece to buy specifically for the purpose. Whichever method, make sure that the timber suits the project you wish to undertake.

Those with plenty of imagination often like to seek out unusually shaped pieces, and may relish the challenge and the unpredictability of the wood. The timber itself can dictate both the subject and the style. A branched piece, for instance, not only suggests a person with upstretched arms but has the added bonus of strength, as short grain is eliminated. Cutting a similar shape from a solid block would also waste a lot of wood.

This approach is especially suitable for stylized or fairly abstract carvings, especially if you do not mind the timber having a few knots or splits (inevitable if the wood is seasoned in the round) –

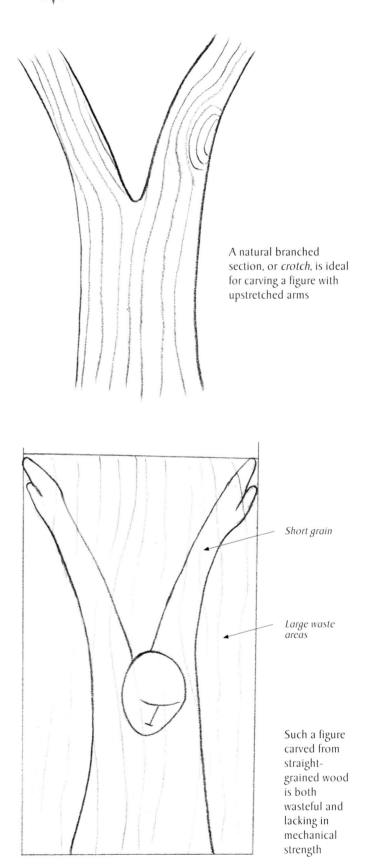

A natural branched section, or *crotch*, is ideal for carving a figure with upstretched arms

Short grain

Large waste areas

Such a figure carved from straight-grained wood is both wasteful and lacking in mechanical strength

39

ABOVE
A discarded gunstock was the source of the highly figured walnut used to carve the fish

RIGHT
Fish
Walnut

indeed, these can be incorporated into the style of the carving. Alternatively, you may have a beautifully figured piece of wood such as walnut or fiddle-back sycamore which suggests the fur of an animal or the scales of a fish, as in the example shown here, which was carved out of a walnut gunstock. Any extra detail carved onto this fish would not only be unnecessary but actually detrimental, as it would obscure the natural figure present in the wood.

Personally, I usually prefer to consider my subject and then find a piece of timber from which to carve it: in this way the design is the dominant force over the material, rather than the timber dictating the design. I like to start with a clean block of wood, with as few blemishes as possible, which is stable and well seasoned so that it will do exactly what I want. This, I accept, is a very safe, unspontaneous way to set about carving, and it is certainly not to everyone's taste.

Whichever approach you prefer, matching the timber to the style and subject of the carving is most important. You must consider colour, figure, closeness of grain and acceptable (or otherwise) blemishes.

Suitable timber for carving

If you have already done a fair bit of carving, you will know that limewood (*Tilia* spp.) is the kindest of woods to carve. It really does almost all a carver can want: it cuts easily, is usually even and free of defects, and takes good detail. What more could you want? Well, for a start, you might find the colour and regularity just too bland, or the wood too easy to carve – almost as if you were cheating. (I rather like this, as I find I can remove so much waste in one go that the subject appears quickly, while still fresh in my mind's eye.)

However, if you want more of a challenge, and love bashing away with a mallet, you can do no better than to get a bit of good English oak (*Quercus robur*). Nothing is more satisfying than watching the medullary rays appear as the wood takes on a beautiful shine straight from the (sharp) tool – certainly no need to sand, and almost no need to polish. The wood is readily available and you can pretend that you are a medieval church carver.

Another wood to consider is steamed pear (*Pyrus communis*, steamed to produce the lovely pink colour), which is extremely close-grained and has little figure – wonderful for carving pigs, crabs or any other brownish-pink wildlife. It can give a rather lurid complexion to people, however. Also try elm (*Ulmus* spp.) if you like a robust wood with a beautiful figure and colour (mid-brown woven with pinks and greens) or, for a rich, dark wood, walnut (*Juglans* spp.) or mahogany (strictly speaking, *Swietenia macrophylla*; but various other woods are sold under this name).

If you wish to know more about specific properties of different timbers, refer to a good manual on the subject.

Size matters

I personally like to carve pieces as large as possible, but usually one is limited to a maximum of 150mm (6in) in thickness, as timber yards are reluctant to dry thicker boards due to the likelihood of splitting. Large figures in churches used to be hollowed out from behind to help prevent this. Although it is, of course, possible to join pieces together, this can cause problems. Firstly, you need a good colour match, and then anything but a perfect joint will show an unattractive white glue line when you carve into it. Also, a change in grain direction on one of the pieces will not only make carving more difficult, but can be distracting when the work is polished, as the light will reflect differently on the separate pieces.

There are times, however, when joining timber is necessary or desirable. You might want to mix timbers for effect, or wish to carve a very large painted figure, such as a ship's figurehead, where the joints will not show. Occasionally it is structurally necessary, as in carving a crucifix, where it is totally impossible to redesign to eliminate short grain. Unless the arms are joined on, so that the long grain runs down the body but also along the arms, the carving is at risk of having the arms and hands break off.

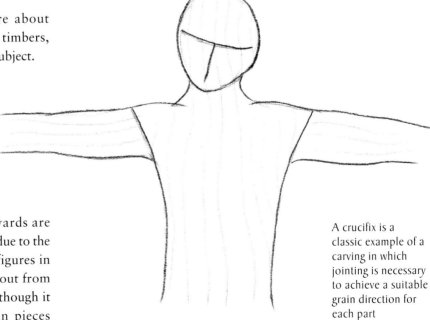

A crucifix is a classic example of a carving in which jointing is necessary to achieve a suitable grain direction for each part

On the whole, carving figures, and especially their faces, is much more successful if the scale is kept as large as possible, but using a single block. It is much easier to carve larger features, and many a small figure is ruined by trying to put minute detail on a face – especially if the carver has limited skill or less than perfect eyesight. It is best to keep detail to a minimum when working on a small scale.

Occasionally, however, a miniature carving is required. It can be a lot of fun to do, but miniatures take a surprisingly long time, and good eyesight and lighting are essential. The little pigs below took me about 10 hours – much longer than I had anticipated – whilst the larger version (described in detail in Chapter 5, pages 98–104) took 24, about what I would have expected for a work of this size and elaboration.

Sow and piglets, large and small versions
Lime

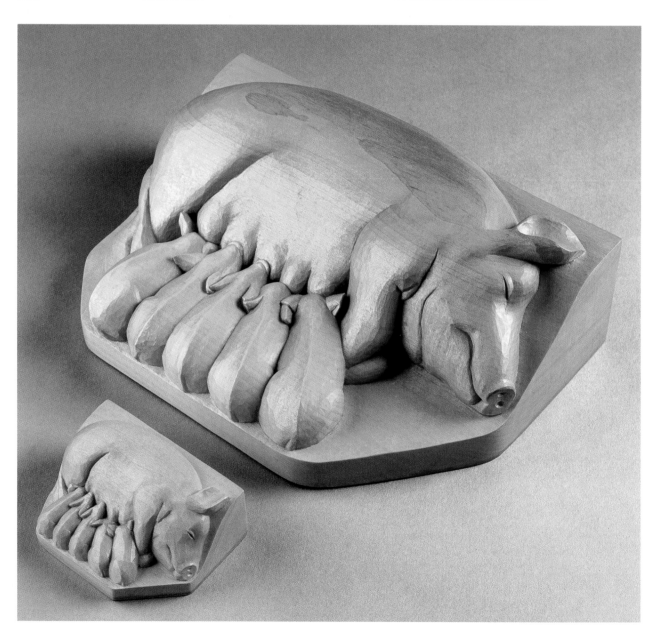

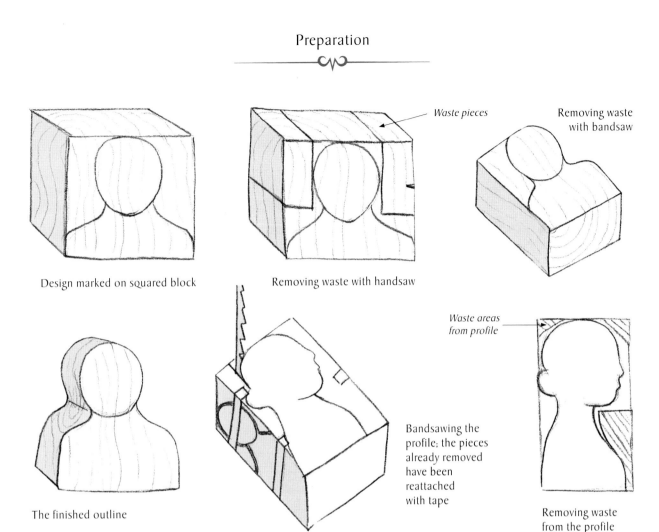

Design marked on squared block

Waste pieces

Removing waste with handsaw

Removing waste with bandsaw

The finished outline

Bandsawing the profile; the pieces already removed have been reattached with tape

Waste areas from profile

Removing waste from the profile by hand

Transferring your design

Before you transfer your design onto your piece of timber, you need to square up the bottom and preferably two opposite faces of the wood; it may be impossible to level the base after you have finished carving, so do not be in such a rush that you omit to do this first. First plane up a face side and then saw and/or plane the end grain at right angles to it, checking with a try square. Next square up the opposite face, so that when you saw around your shape the saw will cut square through the timber. Then transfer the front view of your design by drawing directly onto the wood or by using tracing or carbon paper (carbon is easier), making sure that your design is at

right angles to the base so that your carving does not lean over.

Next saw away the waste, either by using a handsaw to cut away the major chunks, or by bandsawing to your exact line – providing you have squared up properly and your drawing is accurate. Some carvers then reattach the cut-off pieces with masking tape and turn the block on its side to bandsaw the profile. Although I have tried this method, I cannot help finding the result a little alarming, with the nose and mouth running along the width of the face, and prefer to work in from the front only. It is time-saving, however, to saw off large unwanted blocks, such as under the chin, before you begin.

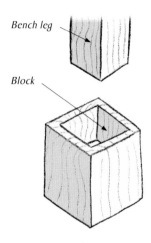

Bench leg

Block

A simple way to increase the height of your bench

Tools and equipment for figure carving

As this book is not really aimed at total beginners, I assume that you already have an adequate number of tools to begin carving with, and therefore I will outline only those which I find especially useful for figure carving.

Firstly, do make sure that your bench is high enough for you to stand and carve without getting backache. I really do not advise sitting to carve, unless you have a disability, as you do not get a good overall view of your work. If you have an old, low school bench, it is possible to raise the height by inserting the legs into mortised blocks.

Next, carving in the round is made much easier if you have a carving stand on which to fix your work. (Allow extra wood at the bottom if you do not like the holes left by the screws.) You can then swivel and tilt your work to allow easy access; I find faces far easier to carve when horizontal, for instance.

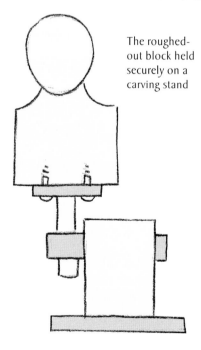

The roughed-out block held securely on a carving stand

Cutting the waste part of the block to an octagonal shape (or attaching an octagonal block to it) allows it to be rotated to eight different positions in the vice

If you do not have a stand, screw or glue a waste piece onto the bottom of the work (with a sheet of paper in between so it can be removed later) for putting in the vice. An octagonal block, made by planing the corners off a square, will allow you to rotate your carving to give a wider range of viewpoints; and remember that you can also tilt the block in the vice.

The toolkit

One of your most important tools is a nice, sharp, moderately soft pencil (2B–4B), which should never leave your bench. As you carve pencil lines off, draw new ones on and you will never lose sight of your image.

The mallet should also be ready to hand, as it speeds up the roughing-out process no end. In spite of advice in some old carving manuals, never use the palm of your hand to strike the tool handle, as this can cause long-term damage; your hands are more important than any tools.

Callipers are a useful addition for checking the dimensions of your carving against full-size drawings or maquettes.

Gouges and chisels

I have a fair number of gouges, ranging from American 'micro' tools through to very large Swiss and Japanese ones, with mainly Swiss and second-hand English tools in the middle. I started with a set of 12 Swiss tools, which I have extensively added to. The Japanese and old English tools were kindly given to me.

RIGHT
My five favourite carving tools, with a small lignum vitae mallet

On the whole, you need only a very few to do most of your carving, and can improvise with the most amazing skill when too busy or lazy to pick up another tool; but every now and then improvisation will not do, which is why having a range of tools is so useful. I have absolute favourites, sometimes irrationally, and can be fickle and change allegiance, but the first tools I get out when starting a figure in lime are:

◆ a 19mm (¾in) German flat gouge
◆ a 32mm (1¼in) old Herring no. 3
◆ a 20mm (¾in) Swiss no. 5
◆ a 10mm (⅜in) Swiss no. 5 fishtail
◆ a 6mm (¼in) Swiss no. 7.

I find the large no. 5 the most useful for roughing out large amounts of lime, although a smaller no. 7 or 8 is better for harder woods. Fishtails are invaluable for reaching awkward places, and the large almost flat tools give a smooth surface when finishing.

Several smaller tools and a skew chisel come into play for detail and features, especially a 4mm (⅛ or 3/16in) no. 8 and 9 and a 3mm (⅛in) no. 4. What is most important is that, however many or few tools you have, each one you use becomes absolutely familiar so that you know what to expect of it and can use it efficiently.

Advice on sharpening can be found in many books, notably the one by Chris Pye listed on page 114. I am therefore assuming that the reader already knows about sharpening (and puts the knowledge to good use), so will only add that it is incredibly important that the bevel at the back should not become rounded or too steep, otherwise you will not be able to produce the large sweeping cuts with the tool which are necessary for figure carving. Oak and other harder woods need a shorter, steeper bevel than pine or lime, however, as the thin edge can easily be lost on the hard timber.

And finally, a little tip when using a mallet and gouge: do not hold them tightly, which strains and tires the hand, but let them do the work and you will be able to work for twice as long!

Mechanical means

As I have already discussed, a bandsaw saves a vast amount of time in preparing your timber prior to carving. Once the block of wood is on the bench ready for carving, however, I use no other mechanical means. Some carvers do not have a gouge in sight, and work purely using rotary bits and sanders; some use a combination of both and others, like me, prefer the direct experience of nothing but hand power, simple tools and a block of wood. Perhaps one should not get too purist, however. Your means of carving should reflect your style of work: a decoy carver would be foolish not to use rasps and files and sand his or her work smooth. If you wish to produce highly detailed work you might want to use tiny burrs in a rotary shaft, while if you work on a massive scale, a chainsaw or angle grinder would make sense. Personally, I only like to work on a scale in which I can comfortably use hand tools.

Finishing

I like to finish directly from the tool, and only sand something if someone wants me to. None of my work shown in this book is sanded, except the fish on page 40 and the pheasant on page 97.

Again, neither a tooled nor a smooth finish is 'wrong', as long as it suits the style of the carving. A tooled finish has the advantage that one does not have to spend laborious hours sanding, but the disadvantage is that your finished tool marks must be strong and look intentional, and there must be no torn or ragged grain in sight. You may also need additional tools for finishing, including a large flat gouge.

A sanded finish can appeal to people for its tactile qualities and the way it brings out the figure in the wood; it is suitable for simple, pure forms. The disadvantage is that it is very time-consuming and boring to do. If done at all, it must be done properly, working through the grades of abrasive papers to a very fine grit – about 600 or more – according to the closeness of the grain of the timber, so that no scratch marks are left. Sanding must never be used as a cover-up for poor carving or blunt tools; you will just obliterate the crisp qualities which add vitality to carving.

When the carving is completed I usually seal the wood with a coat or two of Danish oil and then use a good beeswax polish when dry. Sometimes I just polish, without the oil, as I do not like a high shine on my work; this is purely a matter of taste. Just remember that if you apply as many coats of oil as it usually tells you on the back of the tin, your carving might resemble treacle.

CHAPTER 3
Carving the human head

Girl's head with parrot
Lime

Carving a portrait head can be a very difficult undertaking, especially for the inexperienced: not only must the head be anatomically correct, but it must also be a true likeness of the subject. If you have not attempted to carve a head before, you are probably better off carving a realistic head but not worrying about making it resemble a specific person. In this chapter I will take you through the processes I went through in carving an example head, discussing general points as they arise. I will also do a comparison of two realistic portrait heads, looking at points to consider in carving heads to resemble the model.

Example head

The design

This head is simple in style, with shallow, regular features, and therefore presented no special problems in carving. Even when carving a head at its simplest – especially if you are new to this area of work – make sure that you understand the basic anatomy and proportion of the head before you begin. Be prepared with a good book on anatomy and useful

The photograph which inspired the carving

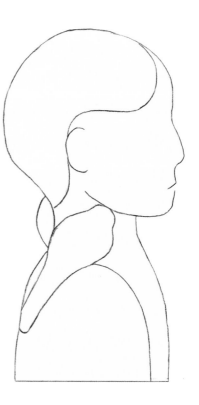

My original drawing of the girl with parrot;
the design was modified to some extent
in the carving

drawings and photographs: do not leave the success of your finished piece to chance. Your initial preparation will not only save time in the long run, but will add direction to your work. For this particular head I used the idea, suggested by the photograph, of a little parrot-like bird sitting on the shoulder of a child.

As I did not, of course, want the ice cream in my carving, and I did not require the finished carving to resemble the child, I simply drew up a quick full-sized sketch of the girl's head with the bird on her shoulder. The bird, to one side of her head, is balanced by a plait across the other shoulder, making a more complete and less stark composition than a portrait head on its own. Although I drew a gap between the parrot and the girl's head, when I came to carve it I closed this gap, making a more solid unit. I decided to have the parrot snuggling into her neck in a cringing manner, with the girl looking down disdainfully from under her eyelids.

The timber

When carving a head, select a nice, clean piece of timber with no knots or blemishes: there is nothing more distracting than a knot which looks, for instance, like a third eye. I tend to favour a bland timber such as lime for figure and head carving, but if you choose wood with a more vigorous grain, make sure that the growth rings do not look like contour lines around high points such as the nose – unless this is the effect you specifically desire. As it is much easier to carve features on a large rather than a small scale, use a piece of wood as thick as you can, about 100 to 150mm (4–6in), and wide enough to give a nice slope to

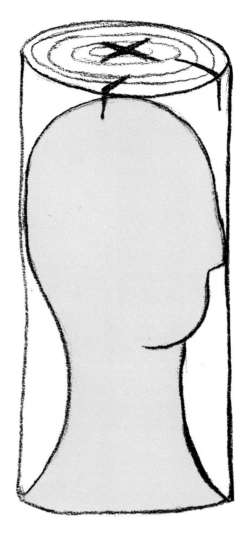

Insufficient depth at the back results in a 'tenpin' head

the shoulder. (You do not have to bother with the whole width of the shoulder, as the carving usually looks in better proportion without.)

Personally I would steer clear of using a complete round log – not just because of the star shake you might encounter in the middle, but because it is all too easy to make the mistake of not leaving enough depth from front to back of the head, so that it ends up resembling a tenpin. Far more depth is needed for the features than most amateur carvers imagine: you cannot simply carve an egg and then stick the features on, as if you were working in clay.

51

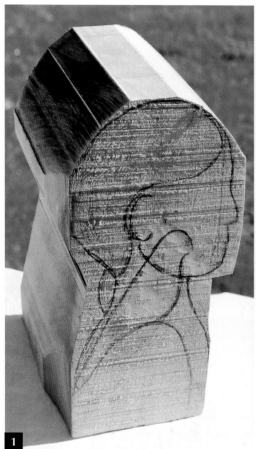

1

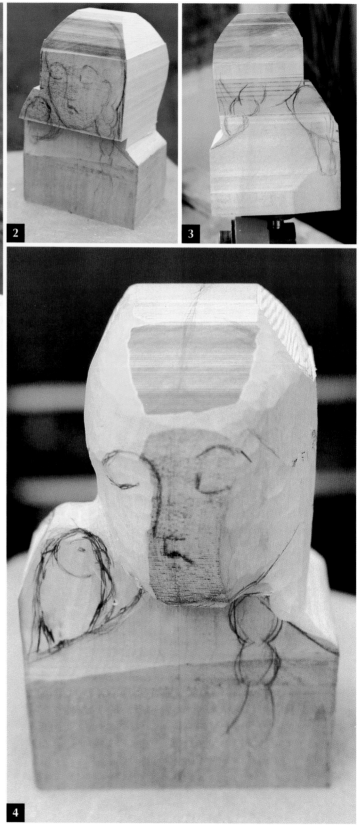

2

3

4

1 The profile bandsawn to shape

2, 3 Front and back views with bandsawing completed

4 First stage of rounding the head

You should, hopefully, be far more successful if you follow the instructions in Chapter 2 and draw up your head onto a flat, planed and prepared piece of timber. In **photograph 1**, you can see that I began by bandsawing the profile and then redrawing the front view so that I could bandsaw away the wood to the sides of the head and under the chin. Do not try to save your initial pencil lines, or to carbon or trace the drawing back onto the surface once curves have been created: you will find that none of your lines match up, due to the elongated surfaces produced by the curve. Instead, draw freehand from now on, measuring if you do not trust your eye. This gets easier as time goes on, until you find yourself totally reliant on your eye and pencil alone. Do not forget always to add the centre line down the middle of the face.

I could alternatively have cut just the front outline and then started with gouges straight away, but logically removing the unwanted timber, block by block with a saw, can save a lot of time. Personally I do not like to bandsaw closely round the features, however.

Photographs 2 and **3** show the front and back views prior to carving.

The carving

In **photograph 4** you will see that a few confident chops with a large, flattish gouge (a no. 3 or 5) have already made the head look fairly three-dimensional. This is achieved by removing the corners of the head, chopping the bird back to shoulder level and taking the sides of the face far enough back to create an area in the middle of the face for the features.

Starting the features

Photograph 5 shows the beginnings of a brow, nose and chin. A prominent nose comes out much further than the brow, but as this carving is to have a small, fairly flat nose, both brow and nose are left equally high.

I started by rounding everything gradually, working the features as a whole, taking care to position them

5

5 The beginnings of the features

correctly in relation to each other as I went. If, at this stage, you keep all your shaping rounded, without digging in deeply and making harsh vertical cuts, you will not have to commit yourself too early and can alter the shapes and positions of features if necessary.

Unless you want to end up with a toothless crone, do not make the common

Correct and incorrect positioning
of the nose and mouth

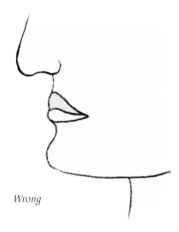

Right

Wrong

6

6 Beginning to
define the eye
sockets

mistake of hollowing out between the
nose and the chin, which has the effect of
making the nose look stuck on and the
chin far too prominent. The chin should be
softly rounded into the neck, rather than
hitting it at right angles. When carving any
head, make sure that you leave enough
wood under the nose for the mouth and
top lip: the top lip comes much further
forward than many people think, with the
sides of the nose set further back into
the face.

Photograph 6 shows a little more
modelling of the features, with the left ear

7, 8, 9 Pencil in the details as you go; shading indicates areas which need to be cut back further

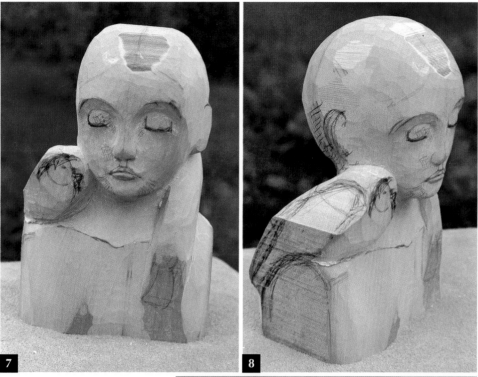

positioned, the central line of the lip and the start of the eyes. The eyes are simplified in this particular head, but remember that every eye is in fact a complete ball set within a socket. If you feel your own you become more aware of this. I tend not to carve eyes in detail until I have more or less finished the nose and mouth, so that I can work back from the high central area and reduce the cheeks, leaving a bump for the eye under the brow.

Photographs 7, 8 and **9** show three views illustrating the necessity of drawing as an aid to carving. You can see that I have used two different drawing techniques: definite lines around the top lip and eyes, and shading to indicate which areas need to be taken down and given more overall shape. At this stage the brow still looks too heavy and prominent, as the forehead has not yet been cut back to provide a hairline.

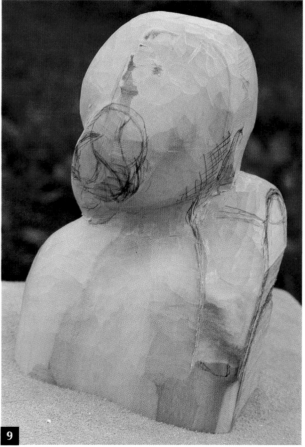

10, 11 Beginning to shape the bird

The bird

The bird, up until this time, has been left rather shapeless and square, but once the chin and neck have been refined, it can be positioned correctly and carved. The beginning stages are seen in **photographs 10** and **11**. If you don't have a parrot-like bird in the house (which I had), a bird book will be necessary. Parrots hold their heads in an idiosyncratic way, and this one, which could be less than friendly, was inclined to nip. I therefore wanted to show a slightly vicious expression on the bird's face, in spite of its apparent affection, whilst the look

on the girl's face shows that she knows just what it is about.

Photographs 12 and **13** show the bird nearly finished. Although the flight and tail feathers are indicated, the bird is very spare of detail, in keeping with the rest of the carving. Guard against putting too much detail into one area of a simple carving, however tempted you may be, as it will not work well as a whole.

Eyes and ears

Eyes especially, whether human or animal, often cause more problems to the

12

13

12, 13 The bird nearing completion

novice carver than anything else, and can make or mar a carving. When you meet someone, it is their eyes that you notice first, and they often give an indication of a person's character. Similarly, in a carving, they should portray the feeling that the carver wishes to convey. Thus your job is not only to make sure that they are anatomically correct, but also that they hold the viewer's attention, as in real life.

Whether you wish to carve in great detail or simply give an indication of the eyes, do not forget that the eye, as previously mentioned, is completely round, set within top and bottom eyelids, within a socket. This can be seen clearly in the drawing below.

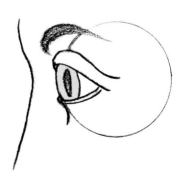

Never forget that the eye is a ball

ABOVE
Girl's head
Elm

ABOVE RIGHT
Girl's head
Lime

In the particular carving we are looking at, the upper lids completely cover the eyeballs, which gives the girl the appearance of looking down under her lids; the bottom lids are merely indicated. These are eyes at their simplest.

If you look at the three carved heads above, you can see the different treatment of the eyes of each. In the elm head a little more detail has been added, as, although she too is looking down, her eyes are open a little wider, showing some eyeball and necessitating more careful carving of the lower lids.

The next two heads, which are discussed in more detail later in this chapter, are more realistic. The girl's head in lime is looking upward with an earnest expression: the lids are carved more vigorously and the irises have been outlined. The man's eyes are deeply set, giving an intense look, rather than the sleepy feeling of the sample head or the elm one. Eyeballs themselves can be difficult to portray, as they are totally smooth and yet the colour change between white, iris and pupil is so dramatic. Some carvers leave them blank, as in the man's head, whereas others do not like to see what they consider to be an expressionless eye, and instead deeply carve the pupil and indicate the iris. There is, however, no

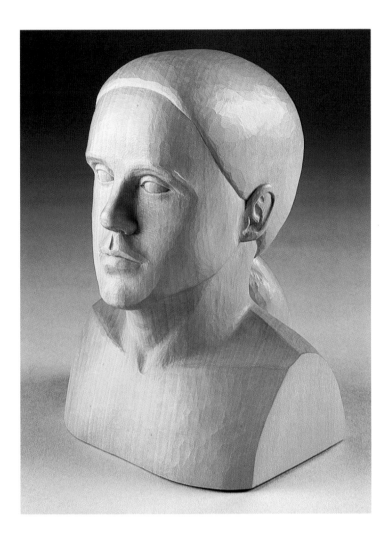

Study the shape
of the ear and its
attachment to the
head

right or wrong; just carve them in a way which seems natural to you, and is in keeping with the style of the piece.

Ears are interesting to carve, as, compared with the other features, they are ridiculously complicated but also (luckily) vary so much in size and shape. Study the anatomy carefully, and make sure that you position them correctly: the position changes dramatically according to the tilt of the head. If you look in the mirror you can see this. As with the eyes, only put in enough detail as goes with the style of the carving. Most importantly, guard against the common mistake of making the ears look stuck on: the front of the ear must

look as if it is attached to, and grows out of, the head.

With the features carved and the bird finished, the head is nearing completion. Apart from cleaning up, the hair is the only area left to tackle. If you look back to photograph 13 on page 57, you can see that the hairline has been cut by reducing the forehead, which had been left oversized for this purpose. I have given her thick hair – which can be well represented by a tooled finish, either cut smoothly or with more of a ripple to it – culminating in a fat plait. Carving plaits can be a bit of a puzzle, especially as they twist over the shoulder, but it is a puzzle which I enjoy;

The finished carving, showing details of the plait

as you can see, all three of the girls' heads shown in this book have a plait. A Barbie doll makes a perfect model on which to arrange a plait to copy as it falls over the shoulder (although it may not be advisable to copy Barbie's proportions!), as a child will not stand still for long enough. Photographs, while useful, are not as easy to copy as a real plait, unless the plait is to hang straight down. Again, when carving hair, consider the style and do not try to cut more deeply than the style of the whole carving warrants.

When I was satisfied with the overall look of the piece, I crisped up the detail and cleaned up the large flat areas with a broad, flattish gouge to give a smooth, tooled finish. How you choose to finish your own piece is, of course, totally up to you; it can look equally striking with anything from a robust tooled finish to a sanded, smooth finish, as long as the treatment is in keeping with the carving. Neither kind of finish, however, will hide bad proportions or torn grain.

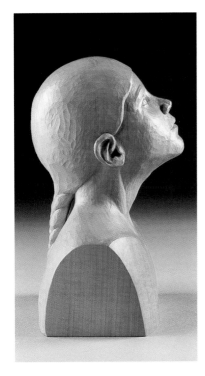

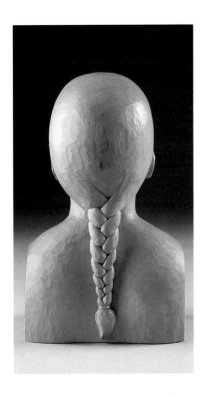

Girl's head, *Lime*

Comparing two portrait heads

If you wish to carve a portrait of a specific person, you need to have clear photographs, or drawings, from the front, side and (preferably) back, with the sitter posing in the position in which you wish to carve them. For these two carvings I used photographs for reference, and drew up outlines to transfer to the wood. Decide on the style of your portrait before you begin; mine were to be traditional representational carvings. It is also helpful if you know your subject personally, so that you can incorporate their character and expression into your carving.

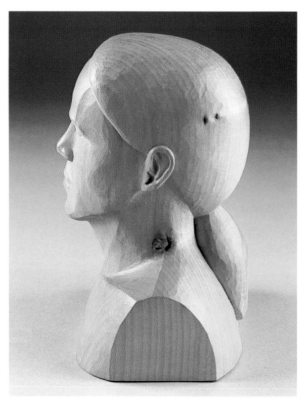

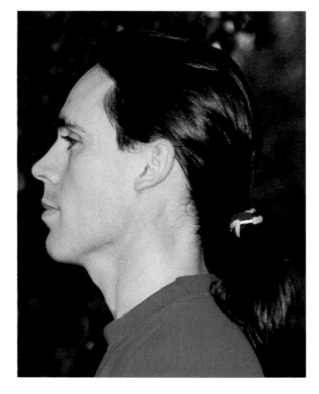

Man's head, *Lime*

Similarities

If you look at the front-view photographs of the man and child on the previous pages, you will see that there are certain similarities between the heads of the two people to be carved. Both have their hair scraped back, both have faces of a similar width and small ears, and both have deep-set eyes under straight brows. Added to which, both heads were to be carved in lime as straightforward busts, with just the head and neck showing.

However, it is the differences which are vital and which must show in the carving: one must look like a man of 30 and the other like a child of seven or eight, with, of course, entirely different personalities. If you really want to capture the essence of a person in a portrait, all the little subtleties have to be examined.

Differences

Firstly, the poses are much more different than they seem at first glance: the man is looking directly ahead at eye level, whereas the child looks upward, as if looking up questioningly towards an adult. (I actually took the photograph from her level, however, so that the proportions would not be distorted.)

Next, although both appear to have little expression, the man's direct gaze gives him an open, honest look, whereas the child looks serious and earnest. The girl's up-tilted head has pulled her neck muscles taut, and her neck – as she is a slim child – is very thin from back to front. The man's neck, in contrast, and in keeping with his sex, is almost as deep as his head.

The side views of the two heads show their different shapes far more clearly than the front, with the child's head much deeper from front to back – a feature which is accentuated by the angle of the head. This angle also makes her ears appear to be set very low and far back, and their shape is almost round, whereas the man's are much higher up and narrower. Whatever the angle of the head, the bottom of the ears will usually sit just above the top of the jawbone.

Incorporating, and slightly exaggerating, individual features in carving – such as the distinct lines from the man's nose to the corners of his mouth – gives instantly recognizable clues as to the identity of your subject. It is helpful to include these characteristics

My working drawing for the girl's head in lime

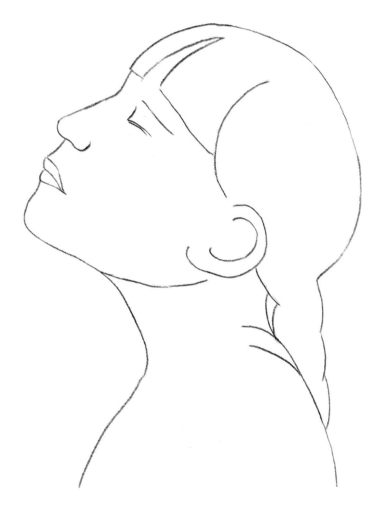

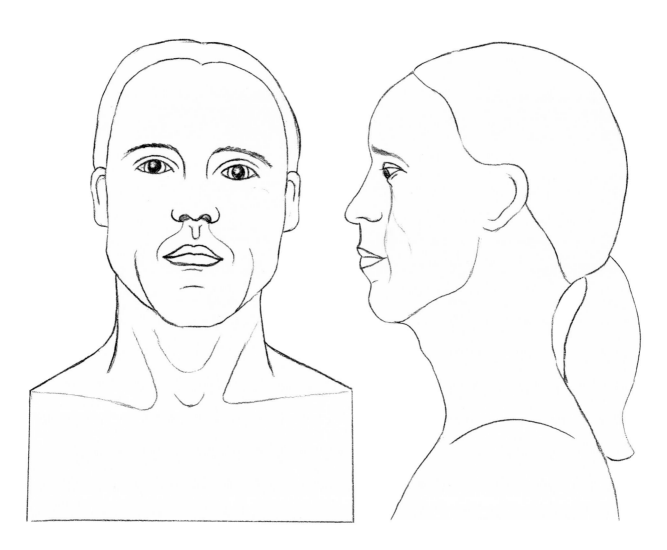

Working drawings
for the man's head

in working drawings, as I have done in the examples shown here; but be wary of overdoing the exaggeration, or you will end up with a caricature rather than a true likeness. All the features are carved as realistically as possible, and therefore with more depth and detail than in the slightly simplified example head.

The finish

I finished the man's head very smoothly from the tool to give a classical finish, which I thought suited his appearance. The child's head is finished with rather more vigorous tooling to go with her more intense, alert expression. The timber I had selected for each, according to the style, also to some degree affected the finishes to each carving. The lime used for the man's head was extremely bland and pale greyish in tone, which gave the completed portrait a stone-like quality. In contrast, the piece used for the girl was much warmer in colour but turned out to be of poorer quality, making a very fine finish unsuitable. A rather unattractive dark stain appeared on the nose during carving but, as usually happens with timber (although unfortunately not with humans), this faded with age.

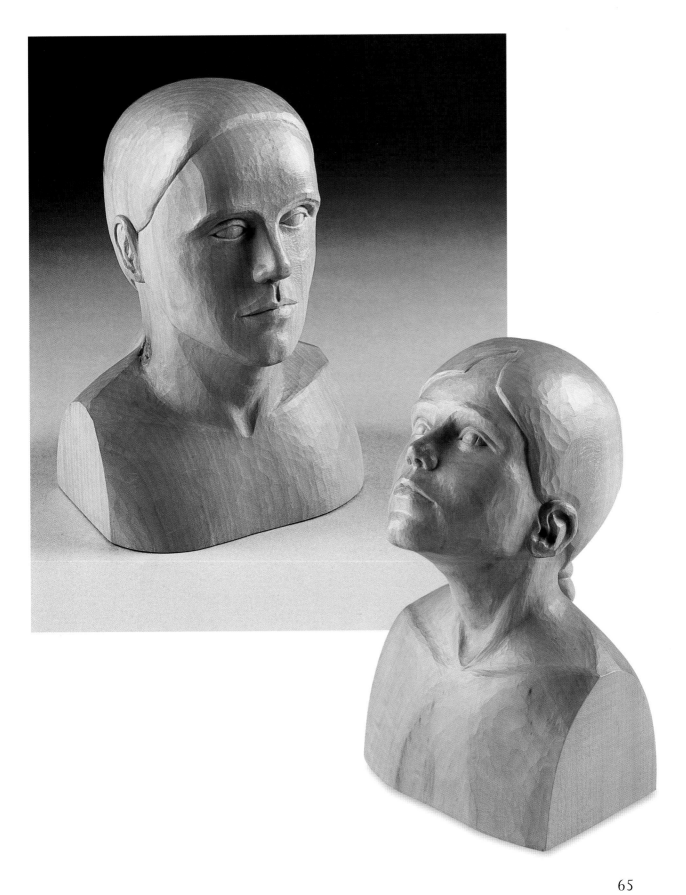

CHAPTER 4
Figures and groups

In Chapter 2 we looked at sources of inspiration for figure carving and at suitable timbers to carve. Direct carving, whether from timber or stone, is a completely different process from modelling in clay: you have to chop away to 'discover' the figure within the wood. It is vital that the figure is in sympathy with the material from which it is carved. Although timber is less vulnerable than pottery, which will shatter if dropped, more delicate and intricate work can be produced in clay. The very structure of timber, so incredibly strong along its length but intrinsically weak across the grain, imposes great limitations. Yes, it is possible to produce extremely delicate, detailed work across the grain, but this seems inappropriate use of wood – what is the point of painstakingly carving a beautiful hand if careless handling can break the fingers off? Wood looks and feels robust, and it seems right that sculpture in this material should reflect its strength. With a little ingenuity it should be possible, for instance, to rotate the hand you wish to carve, so that the fingers run along the grain rather than across it. Always bear in mind the strengths and weaknesses of your chosen medium when visualizing and designing your figure.

The single figure

A figure on its own, especially a nude, is not necessarily easier to carve than a group. The simpler the figure, the more the eye is drawn to the shape and form; therefore all the lines must flow smoothly, especially when carving a nude figure where there is, of course, literally nothing to hide behind. Proportion and anatomy are most important, even if the figure is simplified or the style is intentionally elongated or chunky; every part of the carving must be in keeping with each other. The aims of the carver should be felt through the work and produce a reaction in the onlooker: a work that leaves one cold, or with no emotion, is not a successful carving.

For the figure shown here I posed the child with her hands on her hips to give a feeling of confidence and inner strength. To portray this, the style of the carving is solid, bold and simplified, with no unnecessary detail. I wished this strength of character to be such an overriding force when looking at the sculpture, that the figure's age and gender become more or less irrelevant.

Girl with hands on hips
Lime
Photographs of a real child were helpful at the design stage

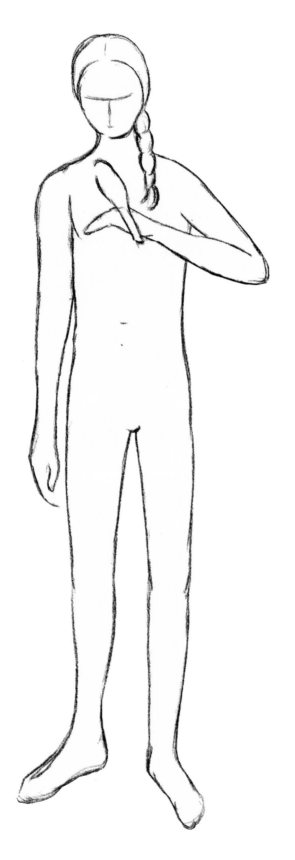

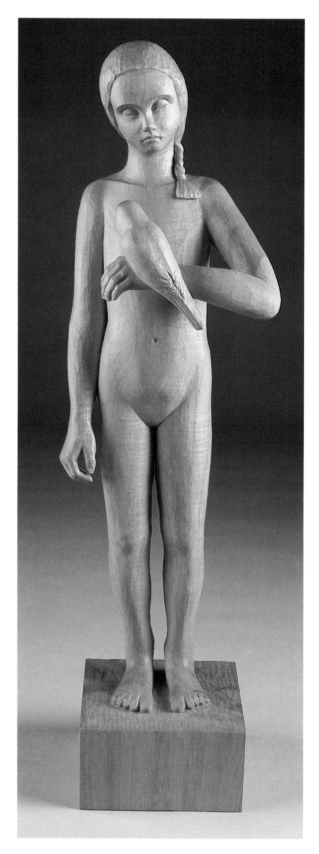

In the next figure (left) I used neither photograph nor scaled drawing, but simply drew a rough idea on a piece of paper and then drew directly onto the wood. In contrast to the ageless feeling of the previous carving, I have exaggerated the leggy, free and unselfconscious stage of childhood. Although the figure is obviously meant to be a little girl, if she were real she would probably be about six feet tall. The previous figure was smooth, spare and slightly stylized, whereas this one, although carved from imagination and not from a photograph, is more realistic and detailed.

You will find that the more you carve, the more you will find a style which suits you and which you are drawn to carving. Both these figures and the detailed examples which follow, although different from each other, share certain characteristics. All are finished from the tool and unfussy in style, and all are carved to portray a feeling of tranquillity: features are reflective rather than animated. Four out of the five examples are holding something living: a bird or a child. This gives a focal point to the work, and also provides me with an opportunity to concentrate on hands, which I like carving, and which should be as expressive as faces.

A detailed look at a straightforward figure: *Standing child with duck*

I had intended to carve this simple shape out of stone (and later did so), but as the weather was cold and I have to carve stone outside, I decided to do the first version in wood instead. I used an extremely hard piece of elm so that I

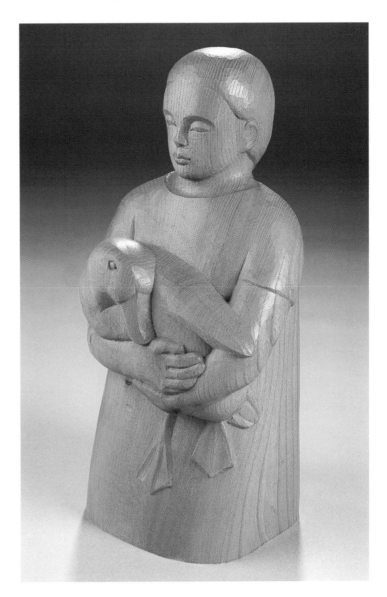

Standing child with duck, *Elm*

FAR LEFT
My original sketch of the standing girl with bird

LEFT
Standing girl with bird, *Lime*

would not be tempted to put in more detail than I wanted – using a very hard wood prevents you from becoming too fussy. Elm would not have suited a more detailed figure, as it has a strongly marked grain which, although beautiful on a simple carving, could be distracting on a more detailed one.

In spite of its simplicity, it actually took 35 hours to carve, due to the hardness of the timber – which must be about double what it would have taken in lime. I did not have to pose the child with the duck, as I had the photograph already and just wished to use it in a simplified manner, concentrating on solid shapes instead of producing a realistic portrait.

I drew a very simple outline of the child, based more or less on circles, squares and rectangles: the dress forming a rectangle, the arms a square and the head a circle.

RIGHT
Working drawing of the standing child with duck

BELOW
The photograph which prompted the carving

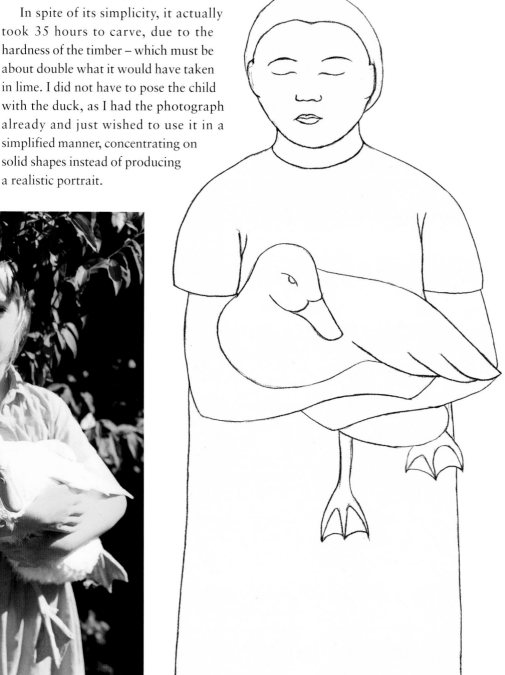

72

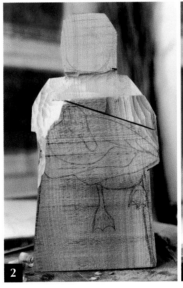

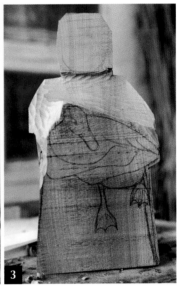

Next, with a handsaw, I cut a diagonal line along the top of the duck's back so that I could chip away this piece of waste more easily (**photograph 2**). To remove this waste I used a small no. 7 gouge and mallet, as the wood proved to be even harder than oak and therefore had to be taken out gradually (**photograph 3**). If this piece had been in lime, I would have used a much larger, flatter gouge and dispensed with the saw.

1 Bandsawing completed

2, 3 Saw and gouge are used to remove the waste above the duck

The figure is of indeterminate nationality and the sex is unimportant, but I wanted it to look as if the child were from sturdy peasant stock. The arms, hands and duck were to be proportionally quite large compared with the child's head, as these had to be the dominant features of the carving, and the shapeless dress was merely to provide a backdrop. She was to hold the stylized duck firmly and confidently so that it looked quite at home in her arms. The carving was to be chunky and solid.

Having transferred my outline to a block of elm 300mm long, 150mm wide and 125mm thick (12 x 6 x 5in), I bandsawed the simple geometrical shape. Then I turned the piece on its side and bandsawed the unwanted chunk away from the area above the duck and in front of the girl's face. **Photograph 1** shows this stage.

In **photograph 4,** both the waste above the duck and the section beneath it have been removed using saw and gouges, leaving a triangular shape from which to carve the duck and the child's arms. All the main areas have been blocked out, but are still square and ready to be shaped in more detail.

4 The area below the duck is removed in the same way

5

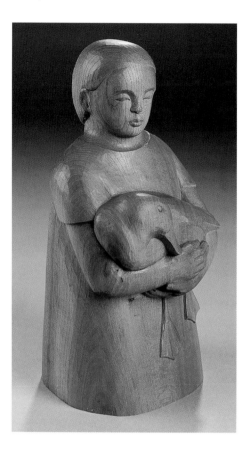

Next the rounding process begins. The simple shift is rounded somewhat but still retains the feeling of a block, which was what I wanted. The arms are released from the sides by cutting back the shift behind them and indicating the short sleeves, and both the girl's and the duck's heads are rounded and separated a little from their bodies (**photograph 5**).

At this stage the figure rather resembled a snowman, so I decided to work on the face and give her a personality. (A more detailed look at carving heads and facial features was given in the previous chapter.)

After redrawing the centre line down the face, I pencilled in where I wished to place the features, which were to be flat and understated, in keeping with the style of carving. The brow and nose were indicated first, the nose being flat and short and the brow fairly heavy. Next I carved the mouth, which is quite full but without much expression: she was to be a phlegmatic girl, coolly presenting the duck like an offering. The eyes, which I like to put in after the other features, look down towards the duck and give nothing away, the blankness of expression being intensified by the lack of detail. The rounded jawline separates the head from

74

the thickset neck, and the hair is tucked behind the simply carved ears and put into a loose plait down the back. The simple neckline of the dress frames the face (**photograph 6**).

The duck is the centrepiece of the carving – more important than the figure herself, who is just the bearer, although her hands and arms create a framework around the bird. It made sense, therefore, to carve these together as a unit (**photograph 7**).

The duck's head is curved round, rather than left outstretched as in the photograph, partly to make a more interesting shape and partly for the sake of strength and compactness. Although there is little detail on its beak or eye, it is making direct contact with the onlooker. Its body is squashed against the girl's dress, barely visible behind her hands except for the simplified wing, which has only a suggestion of feathers. The child's hands were carved flat and fairly large, to give a feeling of security. I placed the

hanging feet tightly against the skirt, rather than cutting them free from the figure, to make the whole carving solid, with no vulnerable parts.

A quick coat of oil and a minimal wax polish brought out the grain without adding too much shine, which would not have suited the style of the carving.

6 The face nearly complete

7 Duck and arms are carved together

75

A detailed look at a seated figure: *Girl with a duck*

As I mentioned in Chapter 2, the photograph on page 31 was a gift for a carver. The child and duck look in perfect harmony. Unusually, the duck is obviously making no attempt to escape from the girl's arms, and so the position of her hands is graceful and elegant, rather than clutching at a wriggling creature. Her tilted head is affectionate and natural. The only changes necessary were to tuck the girl's front leg back and to cover the legs and feet with her skirt so that the lap made a tidier pillow shape for the duck to sit in.

I drew up from the photograph to the size I wanted and then cut the outline out of a block of lime 260mm long by 250mm wide and 140mm thick (10¼ x 9⅞ x 5½in), using a bandsaw.

I had only a front-view photograph, as this was a natural and not a set-up pose, and therefore I had to gauge the thickness of timber I needed by experience and by mentally visualizing it. This was not easy, as I had to estimate how much timber I required for the crossed legs, so I erred on the cautious side and used the thickest timber I had. This proved to be wise, as I did in fact need the whole thickness. If the girl had been standing, I would have got away with using timber barely over 100mm (4in) thick.

LEFT AND BELOW
Seated girl
with duck
Lime

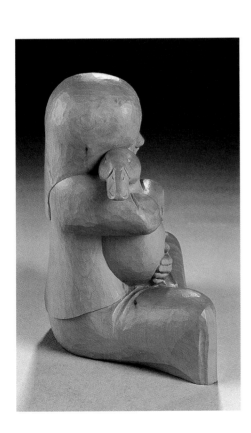

77

As you can see from **photograph 1**, the bandsawn silhouette gave the duck a terrifically wide head and beak, which later gave me the option of positioning its head anywhere along the depth of the carving.

As with all my figure carving, I initially started carving from the front view. The knees are the most prominent part of this carving, so I began scooping out the wood with a gouge and mallet above this area, sloping the wood back to allow for the lower arm being further forward than the upper. This process removed the pencil lines, which had to be redrawn. It is very important to keep pencilling in where the various parts are, when carving in the round, so that at every stage you can see where to position each part and you never lose sight of what to tackle next (**photograph 2**).

By looking at **photographs 3** and **4**, you will see that the main parts have all been more or less roughed out, but kept rounded. There is hardly a definite vertical or horizontal cut in sight. If you work your carving as a whole, using this technique, rather than concentrating in one area or cutting steep and harsh lines, your carving will have more unity. You will not totally commit yourself to the exact position of limbs, etc., until you are sure that everything is in the right place; and, by swivelling the carving around frequently, you can check that all the proportions are correct and that the legs and arms are the right length. Remember: you should still be aiming at gentle shapes and curves that flow together, rather than disjointed elements.

My working drawing for the seated girl with duck, drawn from the photograph on page 31

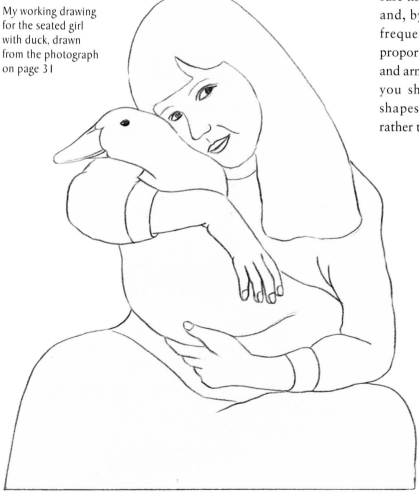

1 The bandsawn outline

2 Working from the front to establish the main planes

3, 4 The main shapes roughed out; they should not be too sharply defined at this stage

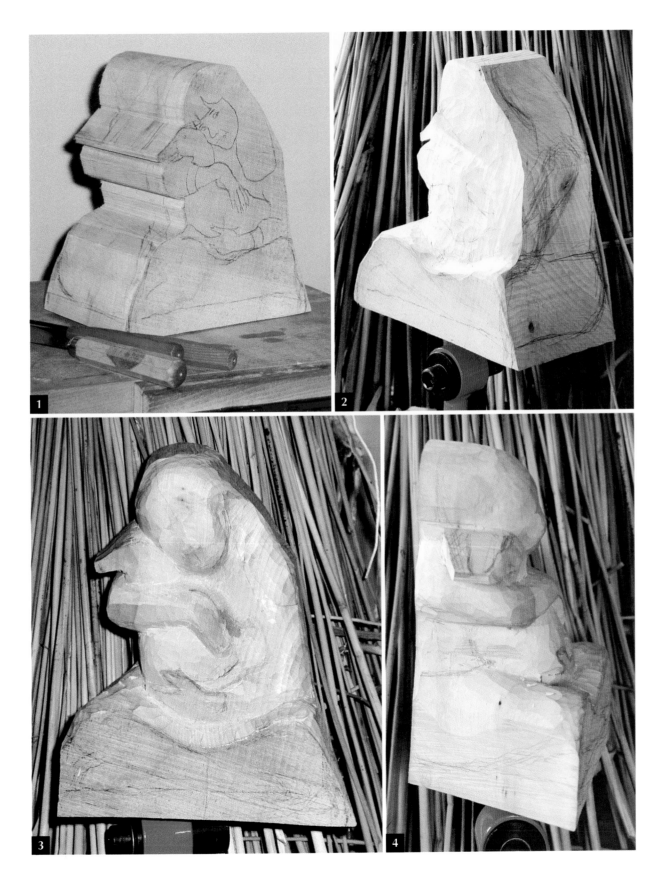

5

5 Refining the shapes; positions of facial features are now determined

6 The heads establish the mood of the whole piece

myself by cutting anything drastically in any one area.

Now everything is in place, the carving is ready for more refining. The outline of the girl's face can be sharpened, with a hint of features emerging, although the chin is still rounded and the neck undefined. The duck has been separated from the main mass and the girl's clothes have a little detail; the hair, jacket and skirt are indicated at the back of the carving. In **photograph 5** the subject is now wholly recognizable, and ready for the next process of adding the detail.

The final stages of figure carving are generally the most enjoyable to do: you know that the carving will work, as the lines and form are correct, and it is just up to you to put in as much or as little detail as you require. This particular carving was to be fairly detailed, as I was aiming at a rather realistic portrait, unlike the simplified carving of the standing child holding the duck – although the carving could have been finished more simply with very little additional work.

As the heads of the girl and the duck and the rapport between them are so vitally important to the feel of the piece, I started by carving them in detail first (**photograph 6**). To counterbalance what could be an over-sentimental and rather mawkish subject, I decided to give the girl a graver, more thoughtful expression than the smile in the original photograph. Her eyes are positioned looking downwards, to the point of being almost closed, to accentuate the unspoken communication between the two, which must be conveyed to the onlooker. In Chapter 3 I have gone into more detail on the mechanics of working the features.

At this stage, you can see that I was also working from the sides, roughly positioning the girl's arms and the duck so that the three-dimensional carving was emerging. Extra wood has been left around the duck's head to allow for adjusting its position, although I have indicated where I wish to place it, and plenty of depth has been left for carving the features on the girl's face. I still have not, as yet, bothered about the back of the carving, as it is straightforward to carve and should pose no problems, compared with the front and sides. Again working the figure as a whole, I gradually slimmed down the limbs, not committing

The girl's hair and clothing have less detail than the more carefully worked face and hands, as they provide the framework or backdrop for the centre of the piece. The hair is carved to more or less resemble a veil, and is just finished with light tool marks as a contrast to the smoother face, whilst the skirt is simply shaped but with some deep gouge marks to indicate the cloth being strung across the girl's knees. The duck's body, too, as it is mainly concealed against the child, is left featureless and without even any indication of feathers. The girl's hands, however, are another matter. Look at the original photograph (page 31) and you will see how one holds and supports the duck while the other falls and rests lightly against the duck's back. The lower hand was quite straightforward, but care had to be taken with the upper one so that it did not look limp and lifeless. The hollow underneath the hand is most important: it creates a shadow which accentuates the curve to the outer edge of the hand and arm.

The resulting carving, due to the base provided by the hidden crossed legs, is compact and sturdy.

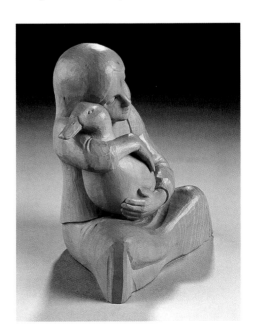

6

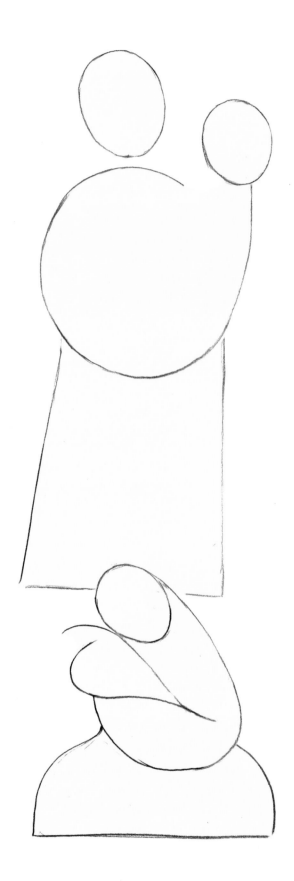

Carving a group

The term 'group' is used to describe two or more figures carved together; therefore the following example would fall into this category.

In composing your study there are two extra points to consider on top of those discussed in carving the single figure. Firstly, whether you carve two or several figures, they should create a unity: make sure that the lines in your composition flow from one figure to the other(s). Secondly, decide whether you wish to portray a feeling of empathy between the figures themselves, which must be apparent to the onlooker. You might not want to carve two people together who look as if they have no more connection to each other than if they were waiting in line for a bus. The two examples of single figures I have looked at each also contained a living creature, and therefore the feeling conveyed between child and duck was a vital consideration in the carving.

If you look at the simplified sketches on the left – one of the sitting girl with the duck and the other of the mother and child which follows – you can see how the curves work together as a whole, strengthening this sense of connection and unity.

By leaning the heads towards each other and emphasizing the close contact, a warmth is created between the figures. Conversely, if you wished to create a feeling of detachment between the figures, they could be carved slightly apart and facing in different directions. Negative or hostile feelings can be portrayed very effectively by the positioning of the figures, as well as by their facial expressions.

If you look at the shepherds from Exeter cathedral shown in Chapter 1 (page 12), you can see that not only has the group been designed well, with a sense of balance, but the figures are also united by a common interest and by their close proximity to each other. In short, the body language of your figures is vital in portraying the feeling you wish to convey.

Mother and child

In this carving I wished to portray the traditional subject of a mother and child, but to place it in a timeless age. The pose is that of a Madonna and Child, but the simple garment and hair of the mother could make it a secular carving also.

Unlike the previous carving, where the photograph suggested the idea, I positioned a real mother and baby into the pose I wanted. This gave me the advantage of being able to photograph from more than one angle. The baby was given an apple to hold, since in many early German limewood carvings the infant (or sometimes the mother) is holding an apple – although I have been unable to trace its symbolism, other than to guess that it might be related to original sin. However, for me it served the purpose of providing an interesting focal point, as well as keeping the baby occupied for the whole duration of taking the photographs.

LEFT
The outlines of the mother and child and the seated girl with duck, reduced to their underlying curves

RIGHT
Mother and child, *Lime*

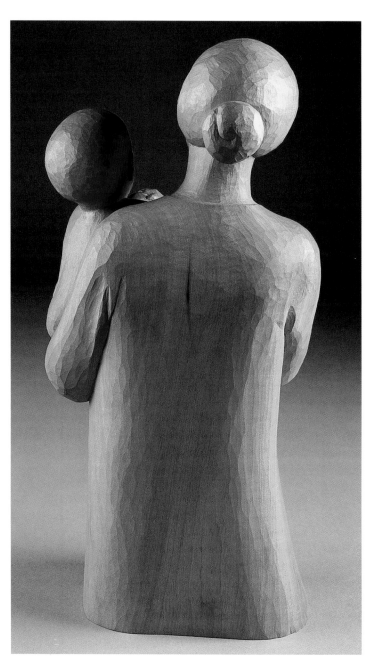

In my first photograph the mother was looking down with her head at exactly the tilt I wanted, and her arms created a nice rounded shape around the child. She wore a shapeless top which (ignoring the inevitable dribble) was loose-fitting, modest and timeless, and could be extended to form a simple robe, whilst the wide sleeves provided some interesting folds. Unfortunately the baby decided to mouth the apple at first, but in the next two photographs held it perfectly. The third photograph showed an all-important rear view of the baby, with its bottom sitting neatly in the crook of the mother's arm. In spite of some clutter in the background, I had three useful photographs from which to make a full-sized outline drawing.

I wished to make the carving as large as possible, but as usual was limited by the thickness of the timber, which was 150mm (6in). The plank was easily long and wide enough, so I scaled up from the photographs, using the side view; although the only complete drawing I bothered to do was a front view, as, in common with many wood and stone sculptors, I like to work in from the front initially. The finished full-size drawing was 230mm wide and 400mm long (9 x 16in), although I extended the length somewhat when redrawing it onto the wood. I drew it up without any need for changes in design, except to neaten the right hand of the mother where she held the baby's feet.

Photograph 1 shows the front view bandsawn to shape, ready to begin.

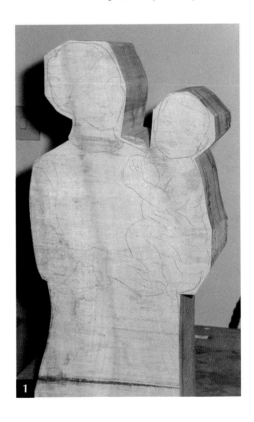

This is always a good time to stop and think: you have done your preparation carefully, squared your timber, transferred and bandsawn the outline and sharpened your tools – yet it is worth standing back for a few minutes to gather your thoughts before beginning.

ABOVE
My working drawing of the mother and child

LEFT
1 The bandsawn block

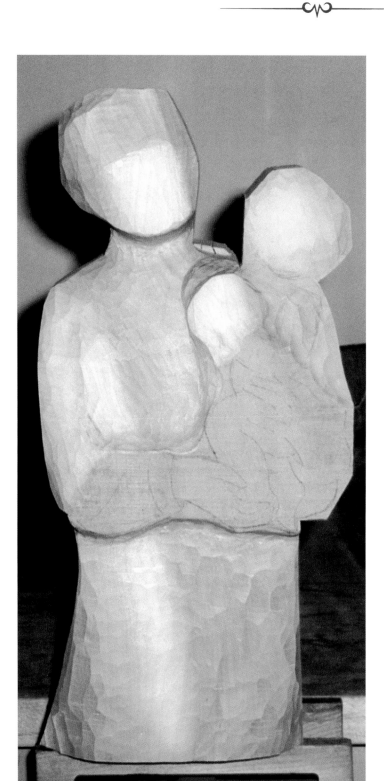

2 The main shapes blocked out

After attaching the carving firmly to the carving stand, I took a good look at my photographs. The pose is a good deal less straightforward than that of the simple carving of the girl holding the duck, as the baby is slightly twisted and sitting to one side of the mother. However, by studying the pictures carefully – especially the side view, which proved most useful – I could begin to think in three-dimensional terms before starting to carve. This speeded up the carving process considerably.

Working from the front, the left side of the baby's body and the mother's right arm and both hands are to the fore of the carving, with the baby's head slightly closer to the front than the mother's. That ascertained, getting to the stage of **photograph 2** can be very quick. Taking back the wood under the mother's arm, and her body above, makes the shape of the carving already recognizable, especially once the heads have been positioned and the space under the chins cut back.

Photographs 3 and **4** show front and side views of the carving half completed. This is the all-important stage when all the major parts are fixed in their finished positions, yet no detail has been added.

The mother is fairly straightforward, as both her pose and her clothing are very simple. Notice that the head tilts towards the baby, whilst the baby's tilts back towards the mother, creating an empathy between them which would have been lost if both heads were straight. The faces have the beginnings of features but no deep vertical cutting, so that I was not as yet committed to their final expressions.

3

4

It is most important, when carving a tilted head, to remember to keep pencilling a line from the centre of the forehead to the chin, so that all the features are carved at the same angle.

The mother's dress was to be extremely plain and loose-fitting, in keeping with her modest and rather solemn, pious expression.

The baby, in contrast to its mother, has a far more complex shape. From the waist downwards the baby is sitting sideways to its mother, but the top half is twisted round to face outwards, with the

3, 4 Two views of the half-completed carving

head facing forward to meet the eye of the onlooker. This twist at the waist creates some very nice deep folds in the skin at the baby's side, which are indicated in pencil, ready to carve; although it also creates a few problems in fitting in the baby's squashed tummy and the farther arm and leg. However, babies are very pliable – look at the incredible curve of the spine in the side-view photograph – so a bit of licence is possible in fitting everything in.

The back of the figure has so far received little attention, as all the action is to the front and side; but, since every part works together as a whole, the carving is now ready to receive its detail.

I decided to leave the detail fairly sketchy for the most part, with nothing too sharp or overworked. The baby's wide gaze is a focal point in the carving, contrasting with the mother's downcast eyes. The shape and position of the mother's hands, as in the previous examples, need to be firm, supportive and expressive. As for the back of the carving, there is little shape to the dress, and the mother's hair is finished with a simple knot.

Unusually for limewood, the timber I used showed a fair amount of figure – so much so that the infant looked alarmingly as though it were wearing a stripy jumper when the carving was first polished – but luckily this has now somewhat mellowed.

This carving took 54 hours to carve, and so, with drawing, bandsawing and sharpening time, about a week and a half to produce.

LEFT
Rear view of the completed carving

CHAPTER 5
Animal carving

On the whole, carving animals usually produces more successful results for the amateur than carving people. The human form is highly complex and, because of our familiarity with the subject, incorrectly carved anatomy and bad proportion are all too obvious. As animals come in such a variety of shapes and textures, many of which lend themselves to simplification, the novice can more easily select a subject to suit his or her ability. Many new carvers are attracted to carving animals which have their lines softened beneath a coat of fur or feathers, partially concealing the structure underneath. However, fur and feathers are not in themselves easy to carve, presenting their own problems. Just how much detail should be included? Do you wish for a highly realistic carving, even though it means laboriously cutting endless grooves with a parting tool? Will you settle for a tooled, impressionistic finish? Or will you sand the whole carving smooth? An elaborate finish will not hide a total disregard of form and structure. Birds tend to present fewer problems, as feathers are often sleek and smooth, so, if you wish, just the tips of the main flight and tail feathers can be picked out in detail.

Personally, I usually prefer not to carve very furry animals unless I have to, as I feel they can be more successfully reproduced in clay. However, most domestic pets are furry, and you may wish to carve a portrait. It could be tricky trying to convince a proud poodle owner that she would be better off with a carved whippet on her mantelpiece than her own beloved creature.

All short-haired animals, such as cows, pigs, greyhounds and goats, are lovely to carve, as their characteristic shapes show well but with just that little covering that the (naked) human lacks. Fish have beautifully fluid, sculptural lines, while crustacea, reptiles and molluscs are best of all for precise carving with a well-tooled finish. Try an armadillo if you love carving detail!

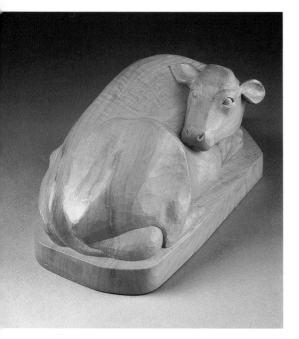

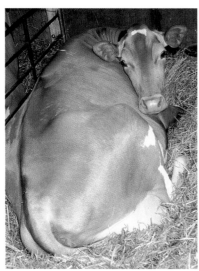

ABOVE
Jersey cow
Lime

ABOVE RIGHT
Devon Red bull
Lime

Comparing styles

Here are three examples of reclining cattle (two cows and a bull), each carved in a different style.

The first, a Jersey cow in lime, is a conventional representational carving. A compact, sculptural shape is achieved by concentrating on the forms made by the twist of the spine, the turn of the head and the back leg. The cow has a smooth tooled finish.

The second, a young Devon Red bull, also in lime, is an example of high-relief carving (as is the carving of the sow and piglets described in detail on pages 98–104). It is more or less representational, but the back blends with the block in which it is set, which emphasizes its solidity, and, although it

Reclining cow
Unidentified hardwood

has a mainly smooth tooled finish, the detail is exaggerated and stylized.

The red cow, carved from a very heavy, unidentified African timber, is a far more angular piece, with little detail and with an emphasis on the prominent bone structure of the animal. The timber is ideally suited to the style of the subject, as not only is the colour correct, but the interlocking grain made it absolutely impossible to produce a smooth or detailed finish without resorting to mechanical means or sanding.

Greyhound head
Lime

Realism and exaggeration

I carved this greyhound head from a little sketch which I made from a print. Although it is obvious what it is, it is also quite clear that if one were to take a measure to the carving, the dimensions would be completely inaccurate.

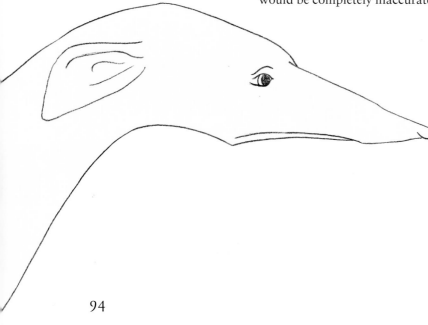

The nose is far too thin, even for a greyhound, compared with the width of the head. By concentrating on my sketch and the image in my mind's eye, I was unrestrained by too much anatomical realism. Instead, I could focus on exaggerating the clean lines of the head, the over-angular jaw and the dog's superior expression.

The crab opposite, on the other hand, is meant to be completely realistic. I picked up an edible crab on the beach, one which had conveniently died at a size which slipped neatly into a large matchbox. I had, therefore, a perfect model from which to take all my dimensions accurately. I doubled the size to 110mm (4⅜in) in length.

Having a beautiful crab-coloured piece of pearwood I eagerly set off, bandsawing my outline and starting to carve from the top downwards.

So far, so good; but this was in my early days of carving and, although the shell and claws went well (I could still hold the crab securely in the vice for both the top and the sides), it was when I tackled the underside that things became tricky. For a start, the more detail I put in, the more difficult it became to hold the work (this was before the time of that wonderful non-slip matting); and also the detail itself was mind-boggling. Not only did the eight legs, each with four sections, fold back on themselves, but huge amounts of cutting through and undercutting were necessary – all by hand, not a power tool in sight. A nice, slim 5mm (³⁄₁₆in) Swiss skew chisel became my best friend in the world. When I had finished I swore that such realism was totally unnecessary, was not art, was only cleverness for cleverness' sake, and that I would never attempt

94

Edible crab, *Pearwood*

1 The basic planes of the crab are set down from the top

2 The edible crab fully roughed out

anything so foolishly time-consuming again. (My resolution was compounded by the fact that it was the only time that I have ever cut myself seriously.)

However, not only did I carve it a companion – the hermit crab, below left – out of the hardest piece of boxwood in existence (so hard that all the legs and claws – which are carved across the grain and should, by the laws of nature, snap off – are as firm as can be), but I have also carved another crab as a commission, cursing the while and again swearing never to do so again. I never have, and my poor little edible and hermit crabs continue to gather dust in my workshop.

Hermit crab
Boxwood

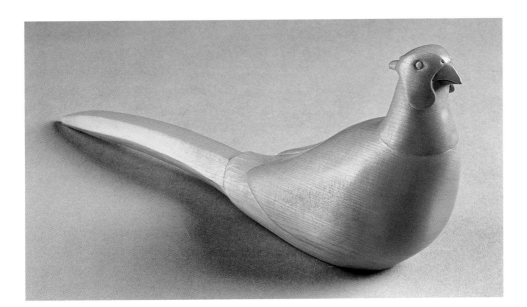

Pheasant
Lime

Texture and finish

Birds are always a popular subject, and many carvers specialize in nothing else. It is possible to carve ducks and game birds which are breathtakingly realistic, especially if they are coloured or detail is added in pyrography, and there are many excellent books on the subject. However, I am not a specialist bird carver and my examples are shown merely to illustrate two different finishes.

The pheasant is completely simple, relying purely on clean lines and outline to achieve the required result, with no detail except on the head. Unusually (for me), it is sanded smooth, and therefore the shape alone catches the eye.

The Orpington chickens, on the other hand, are completely tooled all over and achieve their effect by sheer texture – the shape, in the way of Orpingtons, being ridiculously solid. Although this type of

Two Orpington chickens
Lime

97

A detailed look at a reclining animal: *Tamworth sow and piglets*

As with all my carvings, this is my own work through from idea to photograph, to drawing, to carving. I will describe the methods and techniques that I used, but hopefully you will find it more fulfilling to produce your own one-off carvings, using this as a reference guide, rather than copy directly.

This carving employs the same techniques as, and therefore makes a companion piece for, the bull-in-a-block shown earlier in this chapter (page 92). The sow is actually done in deep relief, not in the round, as although the piglets are completely carved, the mother pig's back merges with the back of the block of timber. This raises the reclining animal to an angle which makes it more easily visible from the front, rather than having to look down at it. It also gives a more compact group, bringing the sow closer to the piglets, than in the stretched-out pose of the real sow and piglets in the photographs.

The subject

Like the bull, this was another compliant poser at a country fair. Because of the confined area, I was not able to get back far enough to photograph the complete pig and piglets in one shot, but the two pictures just about join up with each other and provided all the information I needed.

I then drew up a simple sketch without bothering to draw the piglets in

exaggerated tooled finish is fun to do, sharp tools and a clear understanding of the nature of grain are essential; nothing looks worse or more amateurish than torn grain. Also, do not forget that however much skilful detail or texture you put onto your wildlife carvings, ultimately it is the shape and flowing lines which are your prime concern and denote a good carving. One must guard against the hope that texture will conceal a poor underlying shape. A carving which captures the essence of the bird is far more impressive than one with every feather marked meticulously.

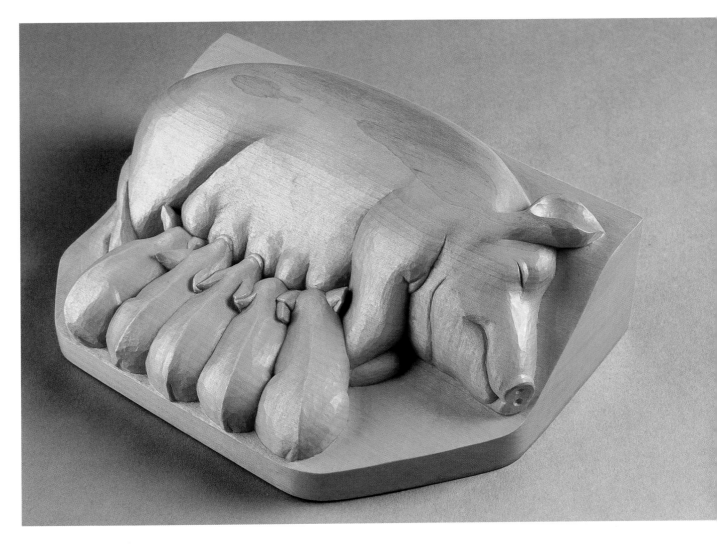

Tamworth sow and piglets, *Lime*

I needed two overlapping shots to photograph the Tamworth sow and her litter

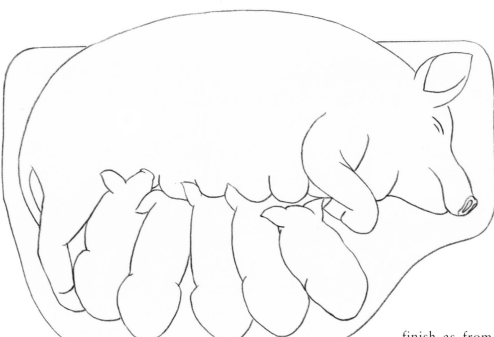

My drawing of the sow and piglets is a little tidier than the original scene

properly, just approximating where they would go, as their bodies have very little detail and are all pushed close up together. I also decreased the number in the litter, as I wanted to fit a row of piglets neatly into the space. Piglets have a habit of lying on top of each other, making use of both rows of teats, but this would create a rather muddled-looking carving and so I kept a single row.

The block

The block of wood needs to be prepared very thoroughly at the beginning for a relief carving: there is no bandsawing to an outline as in carving in the round, only squaring, sawing and planing the piece of wood in readiness for carving down into it. I planed the base, back and sides until completely square, paying attention to the end grain. Do not be tempted to finish the end grain with an electric sander, as you will never get such a good

finish as from a sharp hand plane, although planing is much harder work. I did not bother to square up the front, as I intended to shape this at the end – wishing to cut the base around the finished carving, rather than just leaving it square.

As you can see from the photograph on page 42, I carved both a large and a small version: the large from a piece of lime 280 x 200 x 100mm (11 x 8 x 4in) and the small, just for my amusement, from a little piece 95 x 75 x 38mm (3¾ x 3 x 1½in). However, unless you enjoy carving in miniature, I would avoid working on this scale. Most people seem to favour carving in between these two sizes – a size which seems about right to sit on a desk or mantelpiece. Different points to consider about size include ease of execution, availability of timber and display site, as well, of course, as the wishes of a prospective purchaser.

Having prepared my timber, I drew my outline of the pig on top of the block and then sawed away the waste piece above the piglets, as shown in

photograph 1. This block was big enough, in the larger carving, to save for another occasion.

An advantage of deep-relief carving is that securing the work presents no problems: you can hold it in a large vice, fix it to a carving stand or cramp it to the bench as necessary. I tend to use a carving stand wherever possible, so that the angle of the work can be altered at will.

Starting the carving

First of all I created a nice, gentle, slightly rounded slope from the back of the block down to the lower level (**sketch 2**).

Next I redrew the pig and piglets roughly onto the sloping surface. This must be done freehand, as the slope elongates and distorts the image. Then I roughed out the waste from around the mother and the piglets, leaving a base for them to lie on (**photograph 3**).

If you compare this photograph with the previous one, you will see that I decided to tuck the sow's front leg

1 The carving marked out and the waste block sawn off

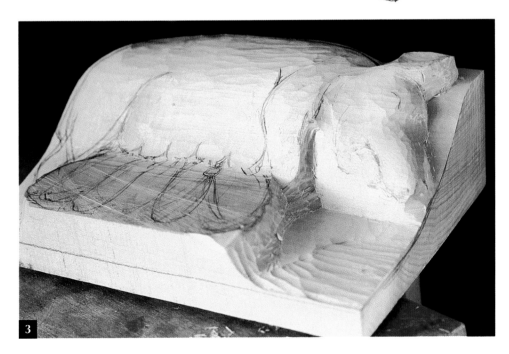

2 The initial slope of the background

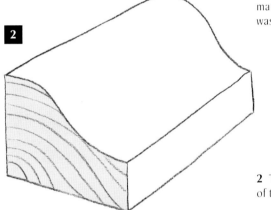

3 The bulk of the waste removed

underneath the first piglet, pulling the group closer together and creating a natural framework between the front and back legs for the piglets to nestle in. Making positive alterations from your drawings or photographs as you go is preferable to following every pencil mark without rethinking anything.

Preliminary roughing out of the sow's legs, which were left higher than her stomach, followed by roughing out of the piglets, put everything in its correct place before any detail was undertaken.

Carving the head

The photographs of the real pig show a creature lying fast asleep, oblivious to her piglets' demands and all the bustle of a busy county show around her; I wanted, therefore, to reproduce her peaceful expression. I started by roughly shaping the head and indicating where the various features would be before concentrating on them individually.

4

The pig's ear is beautifully displayed and very prominent – shaped like an arum lily. Because it is supported underneath, lying against the hay, I could reproduce it by making a generously hollowed shape in the middle of the ear, undercut the sides, and still leave it firm and secure. An upstanding ear would have been more problematic, though not impossible, due to short grain. The band of muscle behind the eye, from which the ear grows out, is a wonderful shape to carve (**photograph 4**).

The snout and mouth need to be worked as a unit as, in common with many mammals (although not humans), the mouth joins into the nose underneath. This can be seen clearly in the original photograph, which gave a good worm's-eye view so I could study the structure in detail. Tamworths have a very long, but to some people's mind not a very beautiful, face.

Attaching the block to a carving stand allows the pig to be upended so that you can look directly down on the face as you carve it. I started with the nose, being careful to make it look as if the snout section really was growing from, and part of, the face. This is more difficult than it sounds. You cannot rely on the colour change from pink to grey, as in the real pig; there is just a subtle, gentle rim around the end. Once this shape is satisfactory, the mouth can be cut, the top lip dividing, and running into, the snout. The lower lip is shaped to sit neatly under and between the two halves of the top one (**photograph 5**).

Pigs are, of course, known for their little 'piggy' eyes, and so these are a minor feature – added to which, my pig was fast asleep (or pretending to be), and so the eye was very simple. All that was

5

6

necessary was a small slit where the eyelids meet, over a slight bump to indicate the eyeball.

The piglets

The piglets fit snugly into the gap between their mother's front and back legs. I carved only five, a small litter for a pig, and could have carved a couple more by making the sow a little longer (mine is perhaps rather shorter than the real one), but I did not want to be carving piglets for ever! Anyway, some of them could have been sleeping a little distance from their mother, as in the photograph.

I began by initially roughing out the piglets as a whole, rather than finishing each separately; because of their overlapping ears, each one is dependent on its neighbour, and together they have to make a unified group with the mother. I then redrew my piglets and cut down between each one to separate them, being careful to leave enough timber for their ears, their snouts and the sow's teats (**photograph 6**).

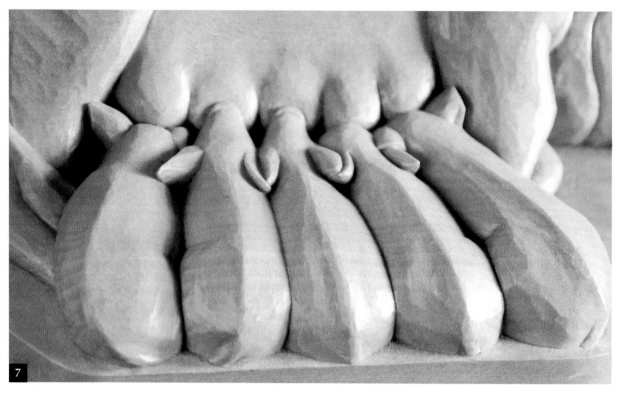

7 A detail of the piglets

The bodies have very little detail, as their legs do not show and even the tails are, for the main part, tucked under their bottoms. I did, however, indicate the prominent backbones and haunches, as piglets are, on the whole, slim, sleek creatures unlike most of their parents. Instead of trying too hard to copy an original in this type of carving, it is better to let your imagination take over somewhat and picture the piglets wriggling and jostling for their own space.

The ears were fun to carve, as they could flop in any direction over each other. The aim was to make the piglets look huddled together, and yet not as muddled as in real life, where it can sometimes be difficult to work out whose ear belongs to whom. If this was reproduced faithfully in a carving, it would merely look as if the carver lacked skill. In the miniature carving, microtools were invaluable for teasing out the tiny gaps between the ears.

The piglets in the photograph are not all suckling, and so mine are not either; if they were, it would look rather contrived. Three have their heads tucked down, either sleeping after their meal or else rooting for the row of teats underneath. The sow's teats have to look both full and rounded, and yet the ones with snouts attached have to look as though they are pushed in like cushions.

A skew tool and a no. 3 fishtail were most useful for getting into the crevices between the ears, snouts and teats (**photograph 7**).

Finally I shaped the base at the front, around the piglets, and cleaned up the whole carving, from the tool only, before polishing. The larger carving took me 24 hours, including preparation, from start to finish, and the smaller 10.

A detailed look at a standing animal: *A cow*

If I could carve only one animal, it would be the cow. Cows have a fine bone structure with the skin both taut and draped around it, magnificent large, kind eyes and a soft-looking nose – plenty to both challenge and entertain the carver. I enjoyed carving this one enormously.

The most important point in selecting your wood for a standing animal is that the grain should run down the animal vertically and not across it. If the grain were to run horizontally the legs would be, in effect, little pillars of vulnerable short grain supporting the weight of the whole body. Even if you succeeded in carving the piece in the first place, the legs would always be in danger of breaking through handling.

LEFT
Correct grain orientation to give strength to the cow's legs and tail

BELOW
Standing cow
Lime

That said, other problems arise from the grain running downwards. To begin with, if you wish to produce a large carving, it is far more difficult to find a big enough piece of timber, as the board must not only be as thick as possible but also as wide as possible, whereas the length does not need to be very great. Also, you have to contend with end grain running the whole length of the back and the stomach, and therefore you cannot finish with long sweeping strokes of the tool along the sides of the animal, as this would be across the grain. However, these are just technical details which an experienced carver can overcome, whereas short grain on legs is an unnecessary structural fault.

Design and pose

The pose of this cow is about as simple as it could be: it is standing solidly, facing straight ahead, with one leg a little forward as if it has just stepped off the page of a textbook. The interest for the onlooker lies in its pure bulk, simplicity and realism, rather than in the more flowing lines of the reclining cows. It is, therefore, essential that it is anatomically correct – although I did leave the legs rather over-thick to increase the feeling of power and size, as well as to provide actual strength. When you look at real cows and horses, it seems miraculous that legs so thin can support so vast a body.

This is a large carving. I was lucky enough to buy a board of lime 150mm thick, 460mm wide and 3m long (6in x 18in x 10ft). This board had, for most of its length, one neat split down the middle, giving me clean, usable timber on either side. One 300mm (1ft) length, however, was completely free of split or blemish. This piece became my cow.

I drew up the cow from animal anatomy books – invaluable sources of reference which enable you to study

My working drawing for the standing cow

proportion as well as showing skeleton, muscles and external features. This was my finished simple outline of the side view, which I drew full size so that I could take measurements from it.

I also looked at live cows and referred to several photographs which I had taken. I strongly advise that, if you wish to undertake a similar style of carving, you do the same, rather than relying on my drawing. (You will find that the British road sign for 'cattle crossing' gives a very good outline, too.)

One of my reference photos of cows

Preparing the timber

Before drawing onto the timber, I made sure that the base was totally square to the sides and completely flat – which involved laborious planing of end grain – so that the cow would stand firmly when finished. Do not wait until the end to do this, or you may find yourself going round from one to the next giving the poor creature shorter and shorter legs – and just imagine the impossibility of planing the end grain on the hooves!

Having squared the timber and transferred the outline, I bandsawed more or less to the line. I then screwed a baseboard onto the waste wood between the front and back legs so that I would be able to fix this board to my carving stand. Luckily, the carving stand took the weight easily, even when swivelled to different angles and with heavy use of the mallet. After drawing my centre line and sawing out the waste between the horns, I was all set to use mallet and gouge (**photograph 1**).

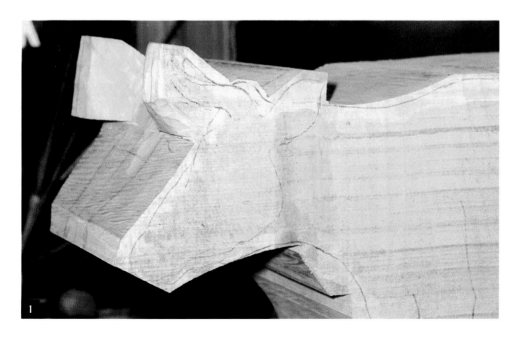

1 Outline bandsawn and waste between horns removed

Plan view of a cow

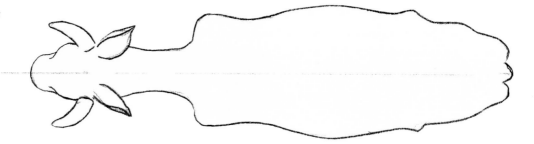

The carving

The first thing you notice when looking at the photograph of the bandsawn cow is that its head is, at this stage, excessively wide compared with its body. If you look at the plan view of a cow above, you will see that the body is very rectangular and the narrower head is supported by a long, thin neck.

The horns and ears are, conveniently enough, more or less the same width as the body, which enables us to make good use of the block of wood. It is logical, therefore, to start carving back from

behind the ears to separate the head from the body and slope the head in towards the nose, leaving the full width for the horns and ears. You will notice, by looking at the left side of **photograph 2**, that this has already started to position the horns and ears at the correct angle, instead of just facing forward, as in photograph 1. The positioning of these very prominent features has to be undertaken with care, as they are crucial to the look of the finished carving. The horns face more or less 45° forward and the ears 45° back, as the plan view of the head shows.

Obviously some breeds of cows have horns at different angles (if they have not been polled), and cows can swivel their ears back and forth, so you can make your own decisions about such details. I have positioned mine to minimize short grain, as well as liking the appearance. They are also left a little thicker than in real life, for the same reason as the legs.

Once the general shape of the head has been established, it is as well to start on the body so that you work the animal as a whole (**photograph 3**). This applies to any figure form, animal or human, and helps to ensure that the proportion of each part is correct and works well in relation to the other parts to produce a harmonious whole. Do not start on any detail until the rough shape is correct.

2 Starting to reduce the width of the head

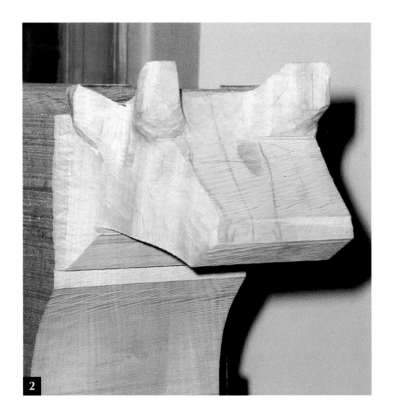

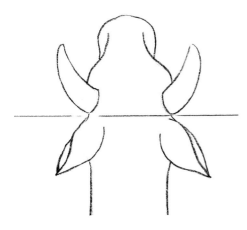

Plan view of a cow's head, showing the disposition of ears and horns

I started to carve the sides according to the plan, cutting vertical channels between the legs and the stomach, leaving enough for the shoulder bones at the front and the roundness of the stomach in the middle (**photograph 4**).

I then rounded under the belly and up and over the back from each side towards the spine, which is prominent down its entire length. **Photograph 5** shows the beginning of the shaping of the cow's back view, back legs and tail. On the right side you can see the corner of the wood which still needs to be removed.

Once the cow has most of its rough shaping, it is time to concentrate on adding more detail all over. I always like working on faces early on, so that the carving develops a character, and I therefore started by putting some life and detail into the features.

3 Body shaping starts with reducing the width of the leg areas

4 The sides are cut back between legs and belly

5 The belly has now been rounded on one side

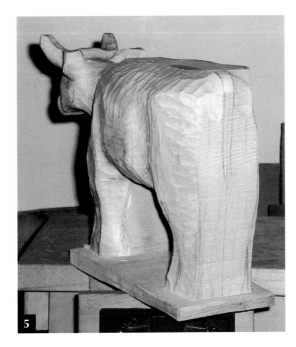

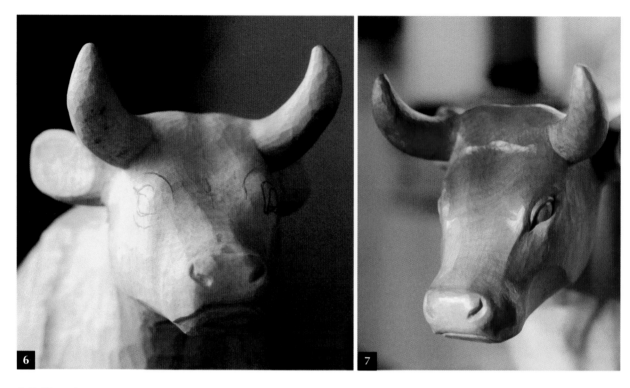

6, 7 Stages in carving the face; the eyes bring the whole carving to life

Cows have generously proportioned, gentle features, and you really need to study a live cow, or your photographs or sketches, carefully to reproduce the structure of the different parts. I usually start with the nose: look at how the nose itself appears as if it is part of the face, rather than looking as if it is stuck on the end. When carving an animal's mouth, do not just carve a line and hope for the best, but observe how the top lip slightly overhangs the bottom one. Eyes, as the most expressive of features, need especial care. In **photograph 6** you will see that I have left low, smooth hills on which to draw the eyes, making sure that they are symmetrical. I have marked lines above and below the eye to indicate the whole eye socket, to ensure that I left enough timber to carve the top and bottom eyelids. The whole eye is sitting in a slightly overemphasized channel to give more life and character

to the face. I also rather exaggerated the jawline for the same reason (**photograph 7**).

Next I worked on the legs, shaping the outsides and then cutting through between them, leaving little hills at the bottom where the cow was screwed onto the base (**photograph 8**). When the legs were satisfactorily shaped, I removed the base and then turned her upside down in the vice while I cut away these pieces and carved her a set of hocks and hooves. She was held very securely in the vice by her sides, so this was also a good position in which to finish the stomach and udder (**photograph 9**).

She needed little cleaning up and finishing, as the tool marks left a pleasing surface – although I did leave the face with a slightly smoother tooled finish than the body, to show up the detail better. A coat of Danish oil and a beeswax polish, and she was complete.

8 The legs nearly complete and the temporary base removed

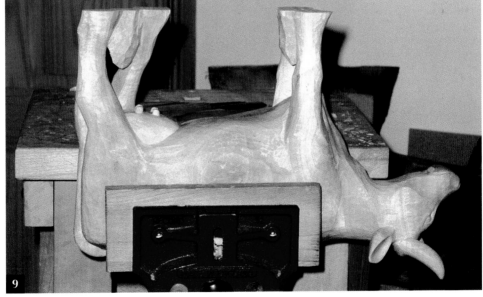

9 A convenient position for finishing the hooves and udder

Conclusion

The aim of any artist or craftsperson is to develop a style of their own. Whether you are a new or an experienced carver, looking at other people's carving and methods of execution, past and present, will help you decide on a direction to take, but it should not make you wish to copy the work of others. Rather, it should spark your imagination towards new possibilities. Although initially you will often be influenced by other people's work, do not let it overpower your own potential. Be constantly aware of, and in sympathy with, your material, your subject matter and your style of work, and let it develop freely.

I have shown you how I go about my carving from design through to completion. I hope this has encouraged you to think up ideas of your own so that you will also feel confident enough to devise and carry out new projects. If, as I intended, you use this book as a guide rather than simply copying my designs, you will gain the added satisfaction of knowing that you have produced an original figure or animal carving. Not knowing whether the work will emerge exactly as you envisaged – as opposed to desperately trying to reproduce the master copy – will add to your enjoyment and satisfaction when the work is finished.

Finally, believe in your ability and start each piece confidently, as if it will be the best piece you can produce – and perhaps it will be.

Further reading

Baxandall, Michael, *The Limewood Sculptors of Renaissance Germany* (New Haven, CT: Yale University Press, 1980)

Chapuis, Julien, *Tilman Riemenschneider: Master Sculptor of the Late Middle Ages* (New Haven, CT: Yale University Press, 1999)

Edlin, Herbert L., *What Wood is That? A Manual of Wood Identification* (London: Thames & Hudson/New York: Viking, 1969)

Ellenberger, W., Dittrich, H., and Baum, H., *An Atlas of Animal Anatomy for Artists*, ed. Lewis S. Brown (New York: Dover, 1956)

Norbury, Ian, *Fundamentals of Figure Carving* (Hertford, England: Stobart Davies/Fresno, CA: Linden, 1993)

Onians, Dick, *Carving the Human Figure: Studies in Wood and Stone* (Lewes: GMC Publications, 2001)

Pearce, Jim, *Wildfowl Carving*, vols. 1 and 2 (Lewes: GMC Publications, 1995 and 1996)

Pye, Chris, *Woodcarving Tools, Materials & Equipment*, new edn. in 2 vols. (Lewes: GMC Publications, 2002)

Schider, Fritz, *An Atlas of Anatomy for Artists*, 3rd edn. (New York: Dover, 1957)

Some places to visit

Barbara Hepworth Museum and Sculpture Garden, St Ives, Cornwall, England

Bayerisches Nationalmuseum, Munich, Germany

Cloisters Collection, Metropolitan Museum of Art, New York, NY, USA

Germanisches Nationalmuseum, Nuremberg, Germany

Henry Moore Foundation, Perry Green, Herts., and Leeds, W. Yorks., England

Henry Moore Sculpture Garden, Nelson-Atkins Museum of Art, Kansas City, KS, USA

Kunsthistorisches Museum, Vienna, Austria

Musée de Cluny, Paris, France

Staatliche Museen, Berlin-Dahlen, Germany

St Paul's Cathedral, London, England

Victoria and Albert Museum, London, England

About the author

Sara Wilkinson was born in 1954 and spent her childhood in the south-west of England. She trained as a nurse on leaving school, and then took a degree in English before studying cabinetmaking and woodcarving at the London College of Furniture (now part of London Guildhall University). The landscape of her early years influenced her love of natural materials and enjoyment of working with wood and stone.

She has exhibited furniture at the Morley Gallery in London, and sculpture and woodcarving at the Celebration of Craft exhibition in Cheltenham. She has published magazine articles on both furniture making and woodcarving.

Sara is a qualified teacher and has gained wide experience in teaching adults and young people. She now lives in Essex, where she teaches and undertakes commissions in both wood and stone.

Index

Index

TITLES AVAILABLE FROM
GMC Publications

Books

Woodcarving

Beginning Woodcarving	*GMC Publications*
Carving Architectural Detail in Wood: The Classical Tradition	
	Frederick Wilbur
Carving Birds & Beasts	*GMC Publications*
Carving Classical Styles in Wood	*Frederick Wilbur*
Carving the Human Figure: Studies in Wood and Stone	
	Dick Onians
Carving Nature: Wildlife Studies in Wood	*Frank Fox-Wilson*
Celtic Carved Lovespoons: 30 Patterns	
	Sharon Littley & Clive Griffin
Decorative Woodcarving (New Edition)	*Jeremy Williams*
Elements of Woodcarving	*Chris Pye*
Figure Carving in Wood: Human and Animal Forms	
	Sara Wilkinson
Lettercarving in Wood: A Practical Course	*Chris Pye*
Relief Carving in Wood: A Practical Introduction	*Chris Pye*
Woodcarving for Beginners	*GMC Publications*
Woodcarving Made Easy	*Cynthia Rogers*
Woodcarving Tools, Materials & Equipment	
(New Edition in 2 vols.)	*Chris Pye*

Woodturning

Bowl Turning Techniques Masterclass	*Tony Boase*
Chris Child's Projects for Woodturners	*Chris Child*
Decorating Turned Wood: The Maker's Eye	
	Liz & Michael O'Donnell
Green Woodwork	*Mike Abbott*
A Guide to Work-Holding on the Lathe	*Fred Holder*
Keith Rowley's Woodturning Projects	*Keith Rowley*
Making Screw Threads in Wood	*Fred Holder*
Segmented Turning: A Complete Guide	*Ron Hampton*
Turned Boxes: 50 Designs	*Chris Stott*
Turning Green Wood	*Michael O'Donnell*
Turning Pens and Pencils	*Kip Christensen & Rex Burningham*
Wood for Woodturners	*Mark Baker*
Woodturning: Forms and Materials	*John Hunnex*
Woodturning: A Foundation Course (New Edition)	
	Keith Rowley
Woodturning: A Fresh Approach	*Robert Chapman*
Woodturning: An Individual Approach	*Dave Regester*
Woodturning: A Source Book of Shapes	*John Hunnex*
Woodturning Masterclass	*Tony Boase*
Woodturning Projects: A Workshop Guide to Shapes	
	Mark Baker

Woodworking

Beginning Picture Marquetry	*Lawrence Threadgold*
Carcass Furniture	*GMC Publications*
Celtic Carved Lovespoons: 30 Patterns	
	Sharon Littley & Clive Griffin
Celtic Woodcraft	*Glenda Bennett*

Celtic Woodworking Projects	*Glenda Bennett*
Complete Woodfinishing (Revised Edition)	*Ian Hosker*
David Charlesworth's Furniture-Making Techniques	
	David Charlesworth
David Charlesworth's Furniture-Making Techniques –	
Volume 2	*David Charlesworth*
Furniture Projects with the Router	*Kevin Ley*
Furniture Restoration (Practical Crafts)	*Kevin Jan Bonner*
Furniture Restoration: A Professional at Work	*John Lloyd*
Furniture Workshop	*Kevin Ley*
Green Woodwork	*Mike Abbott*
History of Furniture: Ancient to 1900	*Michael Huntley*
Intarsia: 30 Patterns for the Scrollsaw	*John Everett*
Making Heirloom Boxes	*Peter Lloyd*
Making Screw Threads in Wood	*Fred Holder*
Making Woodwork Aids and Devices	*Robert Wearing*
Mastering the Router	*Ron Fox*
Pine Furniture Projects for the Home	*Dave Mackenzie*
Router Magic: Jigs, Fixtures and Tricks to	
Unleash your Router's Full Potential	*Bill Hylton*
Router Projects for the Home	*GMC Publications*
Router Tips & Techniques	*Robert Wearing*
Routing: A Workshop Handbook	*Anthony Bailey*
Routing for Beginners	
(Revised and Expanded Edition)	*Anthony Bailey*
Stickmaking: A Complete Course	
	Andrew Jones & Clive George
Stickmaking Handbook	*Andrew Jones & Clive George*
Storage Projects for the Router	*GMC Publications*
Veneering: A Complete Course	*Ian Hosker*
Veneering Handbook	*Ian Hosker*
Wood: Identification & Use	*Terry Porter*
Woodworking Techniques and Projects	*Anthony Bailey*
Woodworking with the Router: Professional	
Router Techniques any Woodworker can Use	
	Bill Hylton & Fred Matlack

Upholstery

Upholstery: A Beginners' Guide	*David James*
Upholstery: A Complete Course (Revised Edition)	*David James*
Upholstery Restoration	*David James*
Upholstery Techniques & Projects	*David James*
Upholstery Tips and Hints	*David James*

Dolls' Houses and Miniatures

1/12 Scale Character Figures for the Dolls' House	
	James Carrington
Americana in 1/12 Scale: 50 Authentic Projects	
	Joanne Ogreenc & Mary Lou Santovec
The Authentic Georgian Dolls' House	*Brian Long*

Crafts

Stitched Cards and Gift Tags for Special Occasions

| | Carol Phillipson |

Tassel Making for Beginners   *Enid Taylor*

Tatting Collage   *Lindsay Rogers*

Tatting Patterns   *Lyn Morton*

Temari: A Traditional Japanese Embroidery Technique

      Margaret Ludlow

Three-Dimensional Découpage: Innovative Projects
  for Beginners   *Hilda Stokes*

Trompe l'Oeil: Techniques and Projects   *Jan Lee Johnson*

Tudor Treasures to Embroider   *Pamela Warner*

Wax Art   *Hazel Marsh*

Gardening

Alpine Gardening   *Chris & Valerie Wheeler*

Auriculas for Everyone: How to Grow and Show Perfect Plants

      Mary Robinson

Beginners' Guide to Herb Gardening   *Yvonne Cuthbertson*

Beginners' Guide to Water Gardening   *Graham Clarke*

Big Leaves for Exotic Effect   *Stephen Griffith*

Companions to Clematis: Growing Clematis with Other Plants

      Marigold Badcock

Creating Contrast with Dark Plants   *Freya Martin*

Creating Small Habitats for Wildlife in your Garden

      Josie Briggs

Exotics are Easy   *GMC Publications*

Gardening with Hebes   *Chris & Valerie Wheeler*

Gardening with Shrubs   *Eric Sawford*

Gardening with Wild Plants   *Julian Slatcher*

Growing Cacti and Other Succulents in the
  Conservatory and Indoors   *Shirley-Anne Bell*

Growing Cacti and Other Succulents in the Garden

      Shirley-Anne Bell

Growing Successful Orchids in the Greenhouse
  and Conservatory   *Mark Isaac-Williams*

Hardy Palms and Palm-Like Plants   *Martyn Graham*

Hardy Perennials: A Beginner's Guide   *Eric Sawford*

Hedges: Creating Screens and Edges   *Averil Bedrich*

How to Attract Butterflies to your Garden

      John & Maureen Tampion

Marginal Plants   *Bernard Sleeman*

Orchids are Easy: A Beginner's Guide to their
  Care and Cultivation   *Tom Gilland*

Planting Plans for Your Garden   *Jenny Shukman*

Sink and Container Gardening Using Dwarf Hardy Plants

      Chris & Valerie Wheeler

The Successful Conservatory and Growing Exotic Plants

      Joan Phelan

Success with Bulbs   *Eric Sawford*

Success with Cuttings   *Chris & Valerie Wheeler*

Success with Seeds   *Chris & Valerie Wheeler*

Tropical Garden Style with Hardy Plants   *Alan Hemsley*

Water Garden Projects: From Groundwork to Planting

      Roger Sweetinburgh

Videos

Drop-in and Pinstuffed Seats   *David James*

Stuffover Upholstery   *David James*

Elliptical Turning   *David Springett*

Woodturning Wizardry   *David Springett*

Turning Between Centres: The Basics   *Dennis White*

Turning Bowls   *Dennis White*

Boxes, Goblets and Screw Threads   *Dennis White*

Novelties and Projects   *Dennis White*

Classic Profiles   *Dennis White*

Twists and Advanced Turning   *Dennis White*

Sharpening the Professional Way   *Jim Kingshott*

Sharpening Turning & Carving Tools   *Jim Kingshott*

Bowl Turning   *John Jordan*

Hollow Turning   *John Jordan*

Woodturning: A Foundation Course   *Keith Rowley*

Carving a Figure: The Female Form   *Ray Gonzalez*

The Router: A Beginner's Guide   *Alan Goodsell*

The Scroll Saw: A Beginner's Guide   *John Burke*

Magazines

◆ Woodturning

◆ Woodcarving

◆ Furniture & Cabinetmaking

◆ The Router

◆ New Woodworking

◆ The Dolls' House Magazine

◆ Outdoor Photography

◆ Black & White Photography

◆ Machine Knitting News

◆ Knitting

◆ Guild of Master Craftsmen News

The above represents a selection of titles currently published or scheduled to be published.
All are available direct from the Publishers or through bookshops, newsagents and specialist retailers.
To place an order, or to obtain a complete catalogue, contact:

GMC Publications,
Castle Place, 166 High Street, Lewes,
East Sussex BN7 1XU United Kingdom
Tel: 01273 488005   Fax: 01273 402866
E-mail: pubs@thegmcgroup.com
Website: www.gmcbooks.com
Orders by credit card are accepted